Everyday Heroes

Everyday Heroes is a wonderful collection of true stories written by health care professionals from across the United States. This book is a special reflection of the tremendous sacrifices, challenges and triumphs demonstrated by today's nurses and health care professionals. *Everyday Heroes* is a celebration of the everyday people who make ordinary moments extraordinary through their heroic acts of kindness, compassion and care. While many of these heroes will never be recognized by the media or the world at large, they are recognized as heroes "one on one" by the thousands of patients and family members they serve over a lifetime. *Everyday Heroes* will make you smile, encourage your heart, and forever transform your definition of the word "HERO."

Every day, inside the walls of hospitals and health care organizations across our great land, there are special people giving of themselves to make a difference, a real difference in the lives of others. They are the people who provide the healing touch to someone who is hurting. Every day, they are the heroes who do the extraordinary. They are the hugs, the hopes, the smiles, the words of encouragement.

About Chris
Thrash

"Chris Thrash's ability to recognize the power and impact of 'Everyday Heroes' creates an enthusiasm that penetrates through hospital walls. Chris is a must-bring to organizations because they are not the same once he shares his stories. Hospitals are never the same once he has been there. Chris Thrash knows the power of 'Everyday Heroes' because he daily walks the talk. Everyone who reads this book will be uplifted to be an 'Everyday Hero' and empower others to do the same. It is a must read."

Juanell Teague, Author of The Zig Ziglar Difference
President, People Plus—Dallas, Texas

"Chris Thrash is our 'Everyday Hero' because he brings energy, enthusiasm, sincerity and a positive attitude to each engagement. Chris leaves our employees with an upbeat message about customer service. He relates so well to audiences. They love him and his message in no time."

Peggy Creany, Director Service Quality
The Methodist Hospital—Houston, Texas

"Chris Thrash is the real deal. His sincerity and genuine belief in what he is doing is obvious to all who meet him and have the pleasure of hearing him speak. Mr. Thrash's presentations were well received and highly rated by all who attended from our CEO to our volunteers. His insight and ability to identify the essence of a service culture and to present it in a humorous way is truly a gift. When Chris worked with our hospital, we immediately saw a difference in everyone's behavior. The best part is that six months later, they still exemplify those same behaviors. We will always be thankful to Chris Thrash for the wonderful improvements he has helped bring to our service culture."

Phyllis Vonderheide, Director Education
Phelps Memorial Hospital Center—Sleepy Hollow, New York

"The more excitement provided, the larger the impact! Chris Thrash has been instrumental in bringing customer service initiatives aimed at increasing our patient satisfaction scores. His contagious personality and energetic speaking abilities are very engaging and thought-provoking. Chris goes above and beyond in creating enthusiasm and energy in motivating our employees to be 'Everyday Heroes' and make a difference in our organization."

Laurie Terry, Vice President Business Practice & Development
San Jacinto Methodist Hospital—Baytown, Texas

"Your presentation was a #1 class act each and every session, and the survey responses from our employees back that up! Thank you for heightening our employees' awareness to customer satisfaction and sharing your true stories and touching moments."

Susan Marks, Director Patient Relations/Advocacy
Humility of Mary Health Partners—Youngstown, Ohio

"What an inspiration! Chris Thrash embodies the true spirit of service delivery excellence. Rather than "talk the talk," Chris "walks the talk." His unique style, creative approach and high-energy delivery left a lasting impression on our employees. Training feedback has been overwhelmingly positive. Attitudes are different. Chris is one of the most polished consultants I have ever had the pleasure to work with. Exceptional!"

Diane Stout, Vice President Business Development
Medical Center of Arlington—Arlington, Texas

"Working with Chris is not only a pleasure, but an experience. What I appreciate is his ability to listen to needs, adapt his presentation and include standards, values and goals in his message. Our employees are still making references to his presentation and message that providing good customer service is not only good for the patient, but can actually make our jobs easier if we all work together. Thanks for the tips and advice!"

Mary Ross, Director Business Development
Memorial Hermann Hospital—Houston, Texas

Everyday
H E R O E S

ordinary people making
ordinary moments extraordinary

C H R I S   T H R A S H

Creative. Training. Solutions.
Midland, TX

Published by Harvington Media, Inc.
4500 West Illinois Ave., Suite 116
Midland, Texas 79703
Phone: 432-699-4383
Fax: 432-699-1411

Publisher's Cataloging-in-Publication Data
Thrash, Chris

    Everyday heroes: ordinary people making ordinary moments extraordinary /
    [compiled by] Chris Thrash. —Midland, TX: Harvington Media Inc., 2003

    p. ; cm.

    ISBN: 0-9741722-0-0

    1. Medical personnel and patient-Anecdotes. 2. Medical personnel-Anecdotes.
    3. Patient satisfaction-Anecdotes. 4. Medical care-Quality control. 5. Medical Personnel, Writings of.
    I. Thrash, Chris

PN6268.M4 E94 2003   2003106666

808.88/3-dc21   0308

Project coordination by Jenkins Group, Inc. • www.bookpublishing.com
Cover design by Chris Rhoades
Interior design by Barbara Hodge
Printed in the United States of America

07 06 05 04 03 * 5 4 3 2 1

Dedication

Everyday Heroes is dedicated to the memory of my niece, Leigha Rose Foley. Over twelve years of her life, she blessed everyone who knew her with her tremendous faith in God, love for people and inspiring courage. In honor of Leigha, a portion of the sale of every copy of this book will be given to Ronald McDonald House Charities for the tremendous assistance they provide to ill children and their families. Our family wishes to express thanks to Ronald McDonald Houses across the nation for their wonderful ministry of love and support they showed to our family over six difficult years of Leigha's battle with cancer.

—*Chris Thrash*

Leigha Rose Foley
February 7, 1984 to
October 15, 1996

Contents

Acknowledgments

There are many "Everyday Heroes" in my life today. I would like to say a special thanks to my wife, Toni, who loves and always supports me with a tremendous strength. I am grateful to my oldest son, Taylor, who has such a gentle spirit and constantly brings a smile to my world. I am thankful to my youngest son, Cameron, who besides giving me my official job title of "preacher of customer service," continuously brings joy to my life. I greatly appreciate my parents, who have been a rock of support and ongoing voice of encouragement throughout my life. I am thankful for my sister, Cindy, who besides being a tremendous asset to Harvington Media (HMI), is a true friend and inspiration every day. I would like to say thanks to my friend Margaret Robinson and the staff of Midland Memorial Hospital, who taught me the "nuts and bolts" of heroic customer service in the '90s. Special love and thanks as well to Jeremiah, Joshua and Sara Foley. I have great appreciation for all of our family and friends with a few in particular who have been closely tied to my personal success—Kerri Day, Keith and Wende McLelland, Kenny Hepner, Peggy Berry, Jon Lindgren, Darrell Dunton, Mel Braneff, Mike Hopper, and Julie Dillman (the Aggie). Most of all, I am thankful that Jesus Christ is the #1 Hero in my life who guides me and gives me the direction I need each and every day.

This book is a collection of inspiring stories that reflect the daily sacrifices of health care workers. Over 3.5 million people work in health care across our country today. These committed staff members give of their time to make quality health care a reality for millions of patients every day. This book celebrates their daily sacrifices—not just as nurses, therapists and hospital staff members, but as heroes... *Everyday Heroes*.

I would like to express my sincere appreciation to every writer who shared their story to be part of this collection. Each of you are heroes in my eyes for the courage, compassion and commitment you represent to the many lives you touch on a daily basis. Thank you for providing such heartwarming stories that will give encouragement and hope to today's hospital workforce.

In February 2000, I produced a video that shares the same title, *Everyday Heroes*. As president of Harvington Media, I stated a specific goal for that video project that I think reflects the same heart behind this book. It is simply this:

"If this book promotes better teamwork on a single nursing unit, produces a few smiles or maybe tears, or lends encouragement to one discouraged staff member, I will feel that *Everyday Heroes* is a true success. Thank you for the wonderful opportunity to share our appreciation for the heroes in hospitals and health care organizations across the nation today."

Chris Thrash, Author

When I
I Grow Up
Wanna be...

"When I grow up, I wanna be..." is a magical phrase all of us probably said many times growing up as children. When I was in third grade, my teacher, Mrs. Blevins, introduced me to a speech competition called "Story Telling." Even though I had always been shy and quiet, Mrs. Blevins picked me to represent her class in the school-wide competition. I was thrilled when I actually won the contest and was picked to represent our elementary school at the district meet. Just when I thought things couldn't get any better, I actually won the blue ribbon at the district meet. I was so proud of that ribbon I wore it to school for many weeks to come. Winning that competition was the first time I really felt like I had accomplished something of great significance. Performing and speaking in front of audiences became my passion that carried me through years of junior high, high school and college speech competitions. Isn't it amazing how someone believing in you at an early age can shape your destiny in such a powerful way? Thank you, Mrs. Blevins, for believing in a shy and scared, nine-year-old boy. That simple introduction to the joy of public speaking has led to a rewarding profession of making people laugh, sometimes cry, but most of all, challenging people to live up to their fullest, God-given potential toward a greater purpose in life. Thanks to a heroic teacher, God has given me the awesome privilege to share hugs, laughter and fun with audiences across the nation as a health care consultant and motivational speaker.

In the fall of 2002, my real professional identity was revealed to me through my then seven-year-old son, Cameron, and his friend, James. Cameron and James were busy playing video games and I happened to walk outside Cameron's bedroom door. I overheard James ask Cameron what his dad did for a living. Cameron replied, "Oh, he just goes all over the country preaching to hospitals." I never really thought of myself as a preacher, but in a sense, I think Cameron probably says it best. My passion for customer service and its role in improving patient and employee satisfaction have earned me the title of "Preacher of Customer Service" in many of my travels.

Throughout this book, several of the authors who contributed their hero stories shared with us what they wanted to be when they were growing up. It is amazing to see how many people always knew they wanted to be a nurse or work in health care. Even those who wanted to be something else as a small child made wonderful ties to how it relates to what they do today.

To those children who bandaged lots of teddy bears, gave candy medicine to their little brothers or sisters, carried around their doctor's bag, or set up neighborhood clinics for wounded pets, we salute you. Thank you for following your dreams and becoming the *Everyday Heroes* you are today.

Leigha's Story

Leigha Rose Foley will always be my "everyday hero." Her contagious laughter, undying courage, and inspiring love for others have served as a constant reminder to me that sometimes our greatest role models come wrapped in very small packages.

At the age of six, Leigha was diagnosed with Wilm's tumor. While the survival rate of this type of cancer is usually very high, Leigha unfortunately had the rare kind of Wilm's tumor that no matter what was tried, the cancer kept raging back like an unstoppable storm. Eventually, at the age of twelve, Leigha would leave this temporary world behind for a better place where there are no tears, no sorrow and no cancer. Over a period of six years, Leigha endured brutal chemotherapy, radiation, a grueling bone marrow transplant and every other horrific treatment in the attempt to find a cure for this beast called cancer.

Did being a cancer patient make her heroic? No. Leigha's attitude toward life is what made her my inspiration, mentor and everyday hero. One of my favorite stories to share about Leigha illustrates the kind of person she was and the wisdom she possessed at such an early age. My sister, Cindy (Leigha's mom), called me one morning from Children's Hospital in Denver, Colorado. I was at home in Midland, Texas, when the phone rang early that day. I didn't know that simple phone call would impact my life from that moment forward.

When my sister called that cold January morning, she told me Leigha had been up all night very sick and had endured almost endless vomiting from a new chemo the oncologist was trying. Having been up all night herself, Cindy was sitting exhausted on the windowsill in that lonely hospital room thinking to herself, "Why me, Lord? Why Leigha? Why did she have to have cancer?" Cindy was in the middle of another all-too-familiar stretch of living in the Ronald McDonald House up the street from the hospital. Once again, it had been several weeks since she had seen her other children, who were at home trying to carry on with "normal everyday life." As a family, Cindy and the other kids had learned the hard way that when cancer strikes, there is no longer such a thing as "normal."

As she sat there blankly staring at the falling snow, Cindy said she was throwing her own private pity party, which to me was certainly understandable given the circumstances. Cindy said the only thing she was grateful for at that moment was that Leigha had finally fallen asleep after such a rough night (or at least Cindy thought she was sleeping). All of a sudden, the sound of a little voice rose from the bed, "Mom, are you crying again?" Cindy replied, "Yes, Leigha, I'm sorry, but I'm just having a rough moment right now. Go back to sleep and get some rest."

After short silence, there came that little voice again with these words: "Mom, can I give you some advice? I think you should try doing what I do every morning to start my day. I think if you would try it, it might make you feel better. Every morning when I first open my eyes, I just thank God for a new day."

That simple story would forever change my perspective on life. If a little girl in that condition who had been through as many things as she had could have that attitude, what problems did I really have? What would I like to nominate as "the issue of the day?"

Sometimes, I complain and worry about finances. I gripe about the traffic as I travel from city to city speaking to hospitals about patient satisfaction. Sometimes, my world seems to come to an end because an airline has delayed or canceled my flight and nothing will ever be all right again, right? In comparison to Leigha's challenges, my problems and worries pale in comparison.

That little voice from the hospital bed was also a very powerful voice. When Leigha spoke, people listened. Leigha had a reputation for being a perfectionist. Everything needed to be a certain way for things to be just right. One time at two a.m., she pushed the call button on her hospital bed and asked the nurse to come down to her room right away. The nurse hurried down the hall and entered Leigha's room asking, "Baby, what's wrong? What do you need?" I'm sure this poor nurse was thinking Leigha needed help to the bathroom or was having an episode of pain out of control, but instead, Leigha's response was simply this: "You know, this room really isn't working well for me. I think we need some things redecorated and reorganized. Could you please move that picture over to that wall over there? And that plant in the corner would really look much better on the windowsill instead of stuck over there."

The amazing thing to me was this: The nurse responded to Leigha with a real sense of urgency that this decorating dilemma needed to be solved immediately. That nurse began to move pictures, change plants around, and rearrange furniture until Leigha was completely satisfied. That nurse was a good example to me of the everyday heroic acts health care workers perform that the world at large may never know about. There may never be a newspaper headline that reads: "Nurse Rearranges Hospital Room Furniture for Sick Child," but I guarantee you, in Leigha's world at that moment in time, it meant everything.

Although Leigha's battle with cancer was extremely painful for those of us left behind, I will forever be grateful for the lessons I learned along the journey. As we traveled to children's hospitals across the nation looking for a cure, I met some of the most amazing people. I had worked in health care for a lot of years. My bachelor's and master's degrees were in health care administration. Over the course of time, I had worked in medical records, radiology, nursing administration, public relations, marketing, and organization development. Surely, I had this thing called "health care and hospitals" figured out. What I learned over the journey of Leigha's illness was that the real heart of health care can never be taught or understood by reading books, writing papers, or even working in a hospital every single day. The following pages tell the story of the real heart of health care: Everyday Heroes.

The Heart of Health Care

The real heart of health care is found in the everyday heroes who give of themselves on a daily basis to make others' lives better. I watched in amazement as a team of nurses would sometimes come into Leigha's room. Kindly, but very matter of factly, they would say, "I'm sorry, sweetheart, but we've gotta poke you again." It was time for another blood draw or needle stick and Leigha didn't have a new arterial line in place yet. I would watch as they would hold her down in the bed with her kicking and screaming, "I hate you! I wish you would all go away! No! No! Please stop hurting me!"

When the trauma was over and the sample had been drawn, I would watch as the nurses left the room apologizing to Leigha for having to hurt her. As they made their way out the door, I would often see a small tear rolling down one of the nurse's cheeks. I thought to myself, what an amazing job. Every day, you get up, get dressed for work, get your own children ready for school, and show up at a place where you get to torture children for a living, have people break down and cry around you on a daily basis, ask you extremely difficult questions, and deal with families who are in the most severe crises of their entire lives. Another perk or job benefit is the opportunity to get really close to people, hold their hand through some difficult days, and share a laugh to brighten their day so that one day, maybe you can say goodbye to them outside the hospital as you send them home to die because nothing else can be done.

One day at a children's hospital where Leigha was a patient at that point in time, I watched as a group of nurses were gathered around a sixteen-year-old boy who was about to be wheeled onto the elevator. They joked and laughed with him and you could see his eyes light up as each one of them kissed him on his bald head and told him to "be good and stay out of trouble." As soon as the doors to the elevator closed and the balloons that had been tied to his wheelchair were no longer in sight, I watched as the three of them huddled there and cried together for a moment. You see, the boy was going home to die because the last cobalt treatment that could possibly work had failed. As they walked back down the hallway toward the nurses' desk, I thought to myself: I guess they get to go back to work now and get close to other kids they may have to say "goodbye" to a lot sooner than anyone wants.

I have learned in more than twenty years of working in health care that some of our country's bravest soldiers are not dressed in fatigues, police uniforms or firefighter suits. They show up every day in hospitals across America dressed in green scrubs, silly tops with cartoon prints or cheerful patterns of another type, or simply in everyday street clothes. These amazing soliders are fighting on some of the fiercest front lines you could ever find. Everyday heroes come in all shapes and sizes, all different personalities and temperaments, but they share one common thing: a willingness to care, share and touch other lives without a lot of recognition or fanfare from the world at large.

This collection of stories portrays their triumphs, challenges, and joys in serving others. These stories tell of a deeper purpose in life, a calling and a commitment to care for people in some of the most extraordinary circumstances.

Teamwork in Crisis

Just prior to publishing this book, I was working as a speaker and consultant with Medical Center of Arlington in Arlington, Texas. I had arrived on Monday morning to speak the entire week (five one-hour sessions a day) to their hospital staff about the importance of customer service and its impact on patient and employee satisfaction. Like many hospitals, they had developed a service theme that was summarized in an acronym. Theirs happened to be STARS (Service, Teamwork, Attitude, Respect and Satisfaction).

The first day of training ended like many others I have conducted at hospitals across the nation. However, the 7 p.m. class would have to be canceled as a severe ice storm had arrived in Arlington just a few hours earlier. The roads were quickly becoming very dangerous and accidents were beginning to pile up around the Dallas area.

The next morning, schools and businesses across the city had closed and many people had no way to get to work. We canceled the first few training sessions of the day as we knew that just providing patient care would be a real challenge. I never knew that what I would witness over the next few days would be a spectacular representation of the STARS philosophy and service theme.

Fearing that if they left the hospital they wouldn't be able to return the next day to take care of patients, nurses spent the night in unoccupied same-day surgery rooms opting to stay and care for their patients instead of going home to their own families. I saw administrators pitch in and help in every way possible on all the various nursing units and in departments that were shorthanded. They even ordered pizza and boxed meals over a two-day period and had them delivered to all the floors, providing them at no charge to staff and families who were staying at the hospital as well. At one point, I was answering the phone in administration so that Sharon, administrative assistant for the CEO, could notarize forms on a nursing floor. I later joked with their administrative team, "Boy, you sure know how to get the most out of your consultants at this hospital. If I can't speak to the staff, you'll just put me to work answering phones." We got quite a few laughs out of that.

I would like to thank Diane Stout, Director of Business Development; Stan Morton, CEO; Cindy Plonein, Chief Nursing Officer; Carolyn Caldwell, and the entire health care team at Medical Center of Arlington for exemplifying the values of their organization in a time of crisis. We were able to rearrange the training schedule and still provide the customer service training for all their staff members. More importantly, however, it was refreshing to see a hospital pull together in such a terrific way to demonstrate Service, Teamwork, Attitude, Respect and Satisfaction all rolled up in a Texas ice storm in February 2003.

It has also been extremely rewarding to see the creative ways hospitals across the nation have taken the "Everyday Heroes" theme based on the video and have incorporated this message into their hospital's culture. One particular hospital that has been a shining example of this commitment to honoring their staff members as heroes has been Trinity Medical Center in Steubenville, Ohio. In the spring of 2003, I had the privilege of meeting Kathy Pasqarella, Trinity Medical Center's Director of Education. I commended her and the Trinity team for the tremendous work they had done to incorporate this message into their hospital's philosophy.

Thanks for the Lift

by Cindy Foley, Sales Consultant
Harvington Media, Inc.—Midland, Texas

"When I was growing up, I wanted to make the world, the whole world, a better place to live. I wanted to improve people's living conditions and to make a difference in society. I wanted world peace (no, I wasn't a Miss America contestant) and I wanted to be involved in the peace process. I would have been an excellent Peace Corps member. Instead, I grew up and became a mother and had children who are making and will make a difference in this world. Today, I have the distinct privilege of raising 'everyday heroes' and I thank God for it."

"Everyday heroes" go unnoticed every day until they save, in some way, you or someone you love. I had an encounter with an everyday hero.

We were in Denver, Colorado. My daughter, Leigha, had been diagnosed with Wilm's cancer. "It shook my reasoning powers—in fact, it shook my whole world." I was in a constant state of paranoia, wondering if my other children had cancer that had not been detected yet. I might take one of them to the emergency room to check for leukemia or I might want one of them to have their annual physical, only quarterly. When I met Dr. Dan, I was having my daughter, Sara, checked for Wilm's.

I took her and her sister, Leigha, to the doctor's office. I told him that I wanted Sara checked for Wilm's cancer. He asked the proper questions, which is not extraordinary. The way he asked the questions was extraordinary, though. He wasn't condescending. He wasn't rude. He didn't give me the impression that he suspected I was neurotic. He checked her with professionalism and concern.

At the end of the exam, we experienced something I'm sure few people have experienced. Dr. Dan looked at my girls. There was my oldest daughter, Leigha, bald, her body thin and frail. He must have seen a little girl whose childhood had been stolen. There was Sara, who probably looked a bit bewildered since she was in a doctor's office being checked for some unknown reason, again. Then, there was me. I must have looked frightened, overwhelmed, and tired. When Dr. Dan looked at us, he had tearful, compassionate eyes. He handed me a twenty-dollar bill and told me to get my girls some ice cream. He couldn't have known for sure what little money we had. He couldn't have known how much we had already been through. Dr. Dan did know this: the girls needed some ice cream and he was buying.

It was not the money that makes this doctor an "everyday hero," although it was, and is, greatly appreciated. What really made him a hero in my eyes is the fact that he had such obvious compassion and empathy.

Dr. Dan, wherever you are, your act of kindness was like a gentle breeze beneath a weary bird's wings. It makes it easier to fly with a little lift. Thanks for the lift.

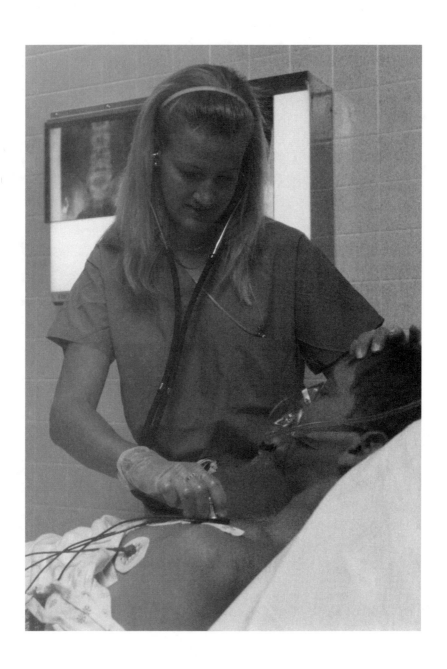

Learning from Countless Heroes on 9/11

by Susan Araujo, Director of Customer Service
Bayshore Community Hospital—Holmdel, New Jersey

"When I was growing up, I wanted to be a nurse because I wanted to be able to help people. My mom was a nurse and she was the coolest person I knew. Today, I am a nurse and a patient representative. I am blessed to be in a position to remind other health care workers why we choose to go into health care. We must always remember that the culture of caring we create today is what we will experience when we ourselves are the recipients of health care."

5

The Changing World

September 11, 2001 changed many Americans' lives forever. We, as individuals and a nation, no longer see ourselves as untouchable. Before this, our view of a dangerous world was strictly seen on a television screen. Bombings in other lands were terrible and caused us grief, but they didn't happen here. Our citizens were immune from the hatred of those who condemn our country because they do not strike here. Our children were free to develop heroes whose major contributions to society were how far they could throw a ball or how fast they could run. Our world changed quickly.

Our children will grow up with new heroes now. Scenes of firefighters erecting an American flag where the World Trade Center once stood, police officers returning to a shattered building to save one more person, never being seen again. A chaplain choosing to place the soul of a dying firefighter before his own life. Yes, our world changed quickly.

Working with Heroes

I had an opportunity to work with other heroes on September 11, 2001. Looking back over my twenty-three-year career in nursing, I now know that I have been working with heroes all along. It is unfortunate that it took an event such as the attack on America to make me see this.

During my nursing career before 9/11, I never really viewed those who work in a hospital as heroes. I practically grew up in a hospital. My mother was a nurse, I was a candy striper, and it was inevitable that I too would become a nurse. I loved the fast beat, never-sleep world of a hospital. It was so vibrant, always moving, always changing, always learning and sometimes reinventing itself.

The inevitable changes in health care were often met with gracious dignity, other times with resistance, but always met. This ability to meet the challenges confronting us daily didn't make us special or noteworthy. The nurses, doctors and support staff are doing what they are trained to do. After all, our job is to save, to comfort, to teach, to reassure, to help. That does not make us heroes. That is the job of hospital staff, isn't it?

The obvious answer to that question is yes. That is the job of every person who has chosen a profession of serving others. But inside of each and every health care worker there is a hero. I would like to single some out now and say thank you.

Thank you to the attending physician who, instead of running home to check on loved ones, came to the hospital to help discharge patients who were well enough to go home and then stayed in the hospital emergency department to help if needed. Thank you case managers and social services for coordinating safe discharges for each patient, making certain that all needs would be met for their continued care at home. Thank you floor nurses who prepared extra rooms and comforted patients and families traumatized by what they witnessed on the news or in reality. Thank you housekeeping staff who uncomplainingly assisted in a quick turnover of emergency room bays so that we could quickly treat and comfort those who were victims of this terrible tragedy. Thank you administration members who put on scrubs and worked hand and hand with the staff. Thank you emergency room staff who worked long hours and held the hands of the injured and psychologically traumatized, ignoring the misplaced anger of family and friends who were so emotionally rattled that they directed that anger toward you. Thank you to the support staff who did all you could to ease the chaos. Thank you to the others who were so vitally involved, our chaplain, dietary, storeroom, respiratory therapy personnel, and countless others. Thank you for letting me see the heroes of health care.

Extraordinary Angels

I would be remiss if I did not also single out some extraordinary angels. Five operating room nurses from Bayshore Community

Hospital wanted to do more than wait for wounded to come to us; they went to them. Their desire to help others outweighed the fear of entering a realm of the unknown and potential danger. They made all of us in the nursing profession proud. The administrative staff later recognized these five nurses.

Other nurses repeated the selfless act of these five nurses all over the Tri-State area and the District of Columbia. We are all humbled when we see the response of nurses in the face of crisis. Nurses are capable of being that extraordinary angel.

Countless Heroes

Our country has found a new group of heroes. Firefighters, police officers, doctors and nurses have replaced ball players and actors. Our children will grow up to hold these noble professions in their rightful place in society. We need to continue to uphold the dignity of these professionals in what we say and do. Countless heroes surround us. We are fortunate. We are Americans.

Just a Job

by Kathy Caldwell, RN, BSN
Cedar City, Utah

"When I was growing up, I wanted to be a writer because I always felt like I had a lot to say, but was too shy to say it out loud. Today, I am kind of like a writer because I still have a lot to say, and the things I say can have an impact on the lives of those I work with and care for."

I never had the "dream" of becoming a nurse like many of my colleagues. I got into it late in life after the end of my marriage. It was a job. Something I could do after two years of school that would allow me to support my children and myself. Over the last eleven years, I've changed my point of view.

It's not the big things I've observed that now make me proud to be a nurse, although they are many. It's the small, everyday occurrences. It's the nurse who works an extra half shift because

9

someone else has called in sick and he can't find anyone else to come in until midnight. It's the nurse who voluntarily takes a patient to chemo treatments on her day off because the patient doesn't have anyone else to drive her. It's the doctor who buys a little boy a brand-new bike because his appendectomy means he missed out on the perfect attendance award at school. It's the nurse's aide who cheerfully comes to work every shift and brightens the lives of all her patients and coworkers, in spite of what's going on in her own life at home. It's the nurse who sits with a grieving family after the death of their child and allows them the time to say goodbye. It's the social workers who come to the emergency department at all hours of the day and night to assist a family whose car has been totaled in an accident and so they are now stranded in a strange town. It's the nurse who washes and curls her older patients' hair for them because she knows that looking better is part of feeling better. It's the coworker who reminded me that people are the way they are in the hospital because they're hurting and would rather be anywhere but here, and that in my twelve hours on duty, I could do something to help make their lives happier. And it's the entire hospital that pulled together a Christmas, complete with tree and presents, in two days for an out-of-state family who through an accident, lost a child and hospitalized the other three children at Christmastime.

So you see, my "everyday heroes" aren't always the ones you see at the scene of a disaster…they're more often my colleagues in the trenches who quietly go about their jobs, being the best they can be and brightening the lives of others along the way. And that's why, for me, nursing is no longer "just a job." It's a privilege.

A Lifetime of Memories

by Kay Hunt, MSN, BSN, RN, Director of Organizational Education
St. Elizabeth Health Center—Youngstown, Ohio

Kay Hunt lived her life caring about others. She was always the first to cheer you on when you succeeded and to give you a hug when you needed it. Everyone who knew her felt she was a mother, a sister or a friend: whatever you needed her to be. Kay was not one to praise her own accomplishments, but no one who knew her could say enough about the way she impacted their lives. At the time of this writing, Kay was the project leader for a nursing accreditation program being sought by her employer, Humility of Mary Health Partners in Youngstown, Ohio. After three years of work, Kay and her team helped the hospital be the first health center in Ohio to receive this high honor. Sadly, Kay passed away from breast cancer eight days after the awarding ceremony. She left behind a strong legacy of love, caring and support. Although we never will be able to forget the pain of her passing, as time goes on, we are able to smile and remember the times of joy we were able to share with her during her life.
We love you and will always miss you.—The Family of Kay Hunt

"When I was growing up, I wanted to be a nurse. I can't even remember a time when I didn't want to be a nurse. Today I am one, and as I look back over the thirty-plus years of my nursing career, I am awed by the number of wonderful people who have crossed my path and the variety of directions my career has taken me.

I have so many wonderful memories to treasure."

Nursing school was an experience like none other—long, starched uniforms and spotless white shoes; the smell of formaldehyde permeating the dorm from the animals we were dissecting; performing procedures on one another; wearing overcoats in the heat of summer to cover up the shorts we weren't permitted to wear in the lobby of the dorm; working all shifts and weekends; becoming that "senior" nursing student and feeling so confident; and then finally graduating and wearing the white uniform and cap of a registered nurse. And my first job—a sixty-two bed general med/surg unit with three and four beds in each room; oxygen tents; trays and trays of "meds" to pass out and shots to give as the medication nurse; working as a team; loving every aspect of patient care—we had so much fun as we cared for our patients. Then, moving into a specialty position in a newly created coronary and intensive care unit—reading cardiac monitors; interpreting EKGs; defibrillating and resuscitating patients; feeling so positive about my career of helping people—I truly had arrived!

I knew that I wanted to teach and so going back to school was necessary. Hard work? Indeed. However, the rewards have been endless. Teaching critical care to more than a thousand senior nursing students at the Jameson School of Nursing over a period of thirteen years—truly the most rewarding job of all. Making another career move into staff development and continuing to be involved with the orientation and continuing education of so many nurses—more and bigger challenges. And then, witnessing the nurses at HMHP striving to be the best and obtain Magnet recognition. Wow!

If I had it to do over, would I change anything? Absolutely not. And I'm sure there's more to come. Through the challenges, the tears, the laughter, the friendships and the many rewards, my career in nursing is the greatest!

All in a Day's Work

by Peggy Scarano, Coordinator Community Services/Fund Development
Little Falls Hospital—Little Falls, New York

"When I was growing up, I wanted to be a renowned physician and cure the masses of all human afflictions. Today, far from conquering diseases and curing all human afflictions, I humbly aim to arouse a simple smile or provoke an inspiring thought through writing health care-related articles for local and area newspapers and by publishing our in-house hospital newsletter."

Four registered nurses from Little Falls Hospital were recently honored for doing what they do best—saving a life! But in this case, they were off duty, enjoying lunch at a popular Utica restaurant.

Heidi Camardello, RN, nurse manager of the surgery

department; Gaylene Charles, RN, nurse manager of the intensive coronary care unit; Rose Flansburg, RN, nurse manager of the emergency department; and Norma Turner, RN, nurse manager of maternity at Little Falls Hospital, were waiting for their lunch when a woman suddenly collapsed. The four nurses responded immediately by moving tables and chairs out of the way, performing CPR and comforting family members. The ambulance arrived and whisked the patient away to a local hospital.

There was no time for lunch now because these women of mercy were on their way to a meeting in Utica. The restaurant owners kindly packed up the lunches "to go" and added a couple of boxes of desserts as a token of their appreciation. It was later discovered that not only was the patient resting comfortably, but she was the mother of a member of the Little Falls Hospital medical staff!

At a special reception held in honor of the nurses, Patricia Failing, RN, director of nursing services at the hospital, commented, "For being at the right place at the right time and for proudly representing Little Falls Hospital by responding with your skilled professionalism, everyone here offers their sincerest appreciation."

A Promise
to My Angel

by Nicole Rese, RN, ICCU
St. Elizabeth Health Center—Youngstown, Ohio

"**I** love being a nurse and feel that I can make a difference through my profession."

On September 18, 1988, the unthinkable happened to my family. My mother suffered a brain aneurysm at the age of thirty-nine. I remember it like it was today. My father and sister went to pick up the rest of the family at the airport to see my mother before life support was removed. I stayed behind, never leaving my mother's side. I was holding her lifeless hand, crying, asking God, "Why did you do this to her?"

A nurse came into the room and asked if she could do anything for me. I said, "Please bring her back to me. I have so much I want to tell her." The nurse held me in her arms and cried along with me. When she finally let go, she looked in my eyes and said, "When children lose their mothers, they gain a guardian angel. Your mother will always be in your heart." The nurse wiped my tears and left the room. I looked at my mother and said, "I love you so much. I will make you proud of me." Six months later, I made a promise to myself and my angel. I would become a nurse just like the nurse who held me that terrible day.

I graduated in May of 1996. It wasn't easy. Many times I wanted to give up. But something inside drove me to keep my promise. I have worked in intensive care at St. Elizabeth's for five years and I find it very rewarding. When I lose one of my patients, I can comfort the family left behind as I can truly feel their sadness. I thank that nurse for holding me that day because through her compassion, I saw my destiny. I love being a nurse and feel that I can make a difference through my profession.

Why I Chose Nursing Education

by Pat McAllen, RN, BSN, MSN, CCRN—Nursing Education
St. Elizabeth Health Center—Youngstown, Ohio

"The best thing anyone can say to me is: I learned so much from you. The greatest compliment I could get would be to have a student go into nursing education so they could make a difference in the profession."

Not long ago, I had an interesting conversation with a group of my nursing colleagues. It centered around the frequently visited topic of what we would have done with our lives had we not gone into nursing. After that litany had been thoroughly exhausted, we moved to the subject of how the attainment of a master's degree in nursing had benefited our careers. One had gone into anesthesia and had never regretted it. She recounted the many reasons why she felt becoming a CRNA was the obvious career path for the MSN.

First, there was the independence and autonomy she

experienced in managing the patients' physiological processes; the chance to work with highly skilled physicians every day; to be on the cutting edge of technology; to have the respect of the OR staff. And, oh yes, the fantastic salary. By working all the overtime hours she can, she makes more than some CEOs and doctors. The rest of us just sighed for the one-thousandth time, wondering why we never chose that path. After a long pause, the one who chose the nurse practitioner route piped up. Although she doesn't make quite the salary of our CRNA friend, she's doing pretty well, thank you; and she gets her reward in giving holistic care to her patients. She loves combining assessing and diagnosing with caring and nurturing. Her patients love her and she goes to work happy and leaves fulfilled.

After another long pause, the group turned its attention in my direction. I was just about to launch into my story when their faces took on the look of feigned sympathy. The questions were the same ones I'd heard for many years now, "Why in the world would someone as smart as you waste your MSN in teaching?" "Do you enjoy making less money than your students as soon as they graduate?" "How can you stand repeating the same stuff over and over to ever-more-clueless nursing students?" Questions like these have always given me reason to pause. But one of the worst comments I ever heard came from a nurse who actually questioned my integrity, saying, "As hard as nursing is these days, how can you in good conscience bring new people into this awful profession?"

That was the last straw. I knew I had to do some hard thinking and come up with some really compelling reasons for why I had dedicated the best years of my life or wasted them teaching nursing. Why did I drive back and forth from Youngstown to Pittsburgh for three years to go to college while my youngest child was only three and while working full time? What insanity would possess someone to take a course in statistics in summer school in between working and taxiing half the neighborhood kids to swimming lessons? Why am I satisfied making a third to half of what my advanced practice nurse buddies make?

These are a lot of good questions that I forced myself to sit down and think about. One thing I've noticed about this fast-paced, frenetic world: people don't take the time to cogitate or ponder or reflect. I don't know if it's because there's no time to do it or because the implications of doing it are too frightening. None of us wants to come to the conclusion that we've made a huge mistake with our lives. But sometimes, if we take the time, we'll rediscover the real reasons we did what we did and, in doing so, rediscover who we really are. So I sat and I thought, and here's why I chose nursing education: I enjoy working with people who still have dreams.

- It's refreshing talking to people who aren't jaded.
- I like… no, I love nursing!
- I enjoy showing students how to do a skill for the first time.
- I enjoy even more watching students perform skills confidently by themselves.
- I'm a gardener and love to plant little sprigs, nurture them and watch them grow and bloom.
- I like to walk through the halls of the hospital and recognize many of my former students and know this place is a quality organization because of them.
- The best thing anyone can say to me is: "I learned so much from you."
- The greatest compliment I could get would be to have one of my students go into nursing education so they could make a difference in the profession.

Money isn't everything, but educators are, in their own way, advanced practice nurses, and I can dream that someday they will be given the respect and compensation they richly deserve. (*I told you I like people with dreams!*)

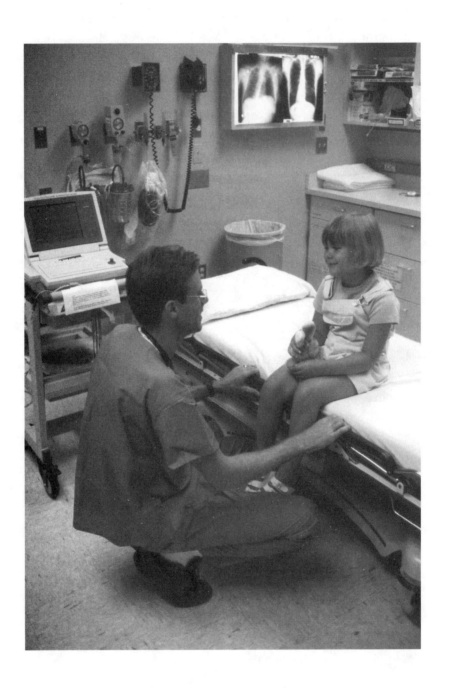

The Electric
Slide

by Dawn DeAna Wilson, Communications Coordinator
Nash Health Care Systems—Rocky Mount, North Carolina

"When I was growing up, I wanted to be an author because authors write stories that can inspire and help others. Today, I am an author, and my first novel, *Saint Jude*, has helped those who are struggling with mental illness."

No victory is hollow, and no defeat permanent. No one can foretell the power of human inspiration, the resolve of determination that leaves its mark on future generations. Such was the case with Lena Galloway, a young mother diagnosed with system lupus erythematosus—a disease that was literally destroying her body from the inside out.

Lena came to Nash Day Hospital's Rehabilitation Department with one goal in mind. It was not a complicated goal by everyday standards. She did not want to conquer Mount Everest or win a gold medal in the Olympic Games.

Her goal was to dance.

When Lena arrived the first day in her wheelchair, she boldly proclaimed to physical therapist Sue Marsigli, "Let's get going, as I have so much to do!"

The odds seemed insurmountable. Sue would be working with a young lady who had lost many fingers on each hand and had below-the-knee amputations. And yet, the goal seemed so deceptively simple—to get up and dance.

"I never knew that this challenge would leave me, even today, with such a beautiful memory of a very special individual who touched many hearts along her journey of life," Sue confessed. "This challenge was met after many hours of blood, sweat, falls and tears. The gym was our dance floor, surrounded with an audience of patients. I put on the music to begin our challenge."

The first step was a tumble that caused an unsettled hush to descend upon the gym. Lena was undaunted.

"No problem," she replied. "Start the music over, Sue."

And when the physical challenge culminated in a rendition of the electric slide, the gym erupted in inspired applause.

"There were tears of joy and sadness as she and I knew her days were numbered," Sue reminisces. "Now that she had met her goal, her hours with me were through. We hugged each other for what seemed like forever as I knew this would probably be the last time I would have the honor to work with this special person who taught me so much."

Lena died shortly after this victory.

A few months later, Sue was teaching an educational program on physical therapy at a local elementary school. Sue asked the kindergartners if they knew what a physical therapist did. One child with big, sparkling eyes and hair styled in cornrows stood up proudly, "Yes, I know," she said. "They help people who lose their legs learn how to walk and dance."

Sue sensed something almost magically different about this child, a special connection, if you will. Sue asked her name. She was Lena Galloway's daughter. Sue called her to the front of the class and together, moving to a melody etched silently inside their memories, they danced to the electric slide.

A Nurse's Prayer

by Kathy Machingo, RN, BSN, Heart and Vascular Services
St. Elizabeth Health Center—Youngstown, Ohio

"When I was growing up, I wanted to be a nurse so I could help people. Today, I am a nurse, and it warms my soul to holistically enhance the quality of life of each person I encounter."

When I was twelve, I was a candy striper at the old St. Joseph Riverside Hospital. I found a funny-looking ice pitcher and unknowingly filled some guy's empty urinal with ice water and that was the beginning of my "live and learn" love for nursing.

It didn't come easy for me, though. After high school, I entered the Youngstown State University associate degree program. My first quarter didn't go well so I dropped out. Three years later, I applied to Choffin in the hopes of becoming an LPN. After being placed on a waiting list, I returned to YSU and pursued an associate degree in nursing.

I remember vividly Diane Smolen, one of my favorite nursing instructors. Diane told us if we treated our patients like they were our family, we would never provide anything but the best care from the heart.

I went to work at Warren General Hospital and began in medical/surgical. Having a deep compassion for my patients, I did everything I could to please them. I recall helping a family smuggle a small gray poodle in one Sunday morning to grant a dying man's last wish… to see his dog one last time. He died four days later.

I returned to Penn State Shenango campus to pursue my BSN while continuing to juggle the roles of mother, wife and full-time nurse. My experiences as a nurse kept building.

One New Year's Eve, I began to care for a woman who was critically injured in an accident. Come to find out, her family all lived out of state. I grew attached to her and followed her recovery throughout her hospital stay. A good friend of mine and I would do things like wash her hair and trim her nails before we'd leave for the day. We befriended her and she kept in touch by mail for seven years until she passed away.

I believe that every encounter is a gift, each patient a privilege to know and care for. Some we know better than others; some we barely know at all. We are all just passing through this life and if there is a kindness I can show, a touch that will comfort, or knowledge I can share that will help a patient...then I am the one blessed…blessed to be there for them at their moment of need.

I came to nursing out of an internal sense of duty…and I stay out of a sense of pride, accomplishment and passion for my profession. I would like to share a prayer from a friend of my family who began her nursing career in the late 1940s.

"A NURSE'S PRAYER"
"Let me dedicate my life today to care for those
who come my way.
Let me touch each one with healing hand and the
gentle care for which I stand.
And then tonight when day is done, Oh let me rest in
peace if I helped just one."

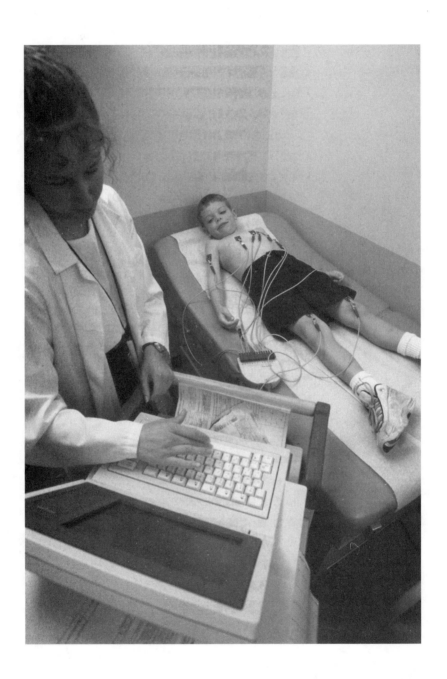

Special
Request

by Mary Ann Board, LMSW-ACP
The Methodist Hospital—Houston, Texas

"When I was growing up, I wanted to be a teacher because I wanted to be a positive influence in the lives of youth. Today, I am like a teacher because as a medical social worker, I teach patients and families about their discharge options and eligibility for benefits. Hopefully, I help them grow and understand our complex medical system."

I am a medical social worker at the Methodist Hospital in Houston, Texas, and I recently received an unusual request from a patient's family. The patient was to be discharged home with hospice care in just a few days. Before she left the hospital, the family surprised her with a special birthday party in her room. The day of the celebration, the patient's daughter approached me and said, "Someone told me that you sing in your church choir. Would you sing two of my mother's favorite hymns at her birthday party this afternoon? She loves 'The Old Rugged Cross' and 'How Great Thou Art.'"

I paled at the thought. Yes, I do sing in my church choir, but I'm a blender, not a soloist. I quickly agreed though, and then immediately began to problem-solve my predicament. First, I called the chaplain's office, hoping to get a volunteer singer. If no one was available, I thought, I could at least request prayers. Fortunately, the hospital had recently accepted some students for the chaplaincy program and one of them could sing! He told me his father had recently died and that he and his son had been at the bedside singing his father's favorite hymns. He would be happy to sing for my patient.

Then I remembered a social work colleague who also sings in her church choir *and* is a soprano soloist. I called her up and explained the situation. Fortunately, she was not conducting a group at that time and readily accepted the challenge.

At the appointed time for the party, our singing trio arrived in the patient's room. Children, grandchildren and great-grandchildren were gathered around the bed. The patient was alert and reclined in her bed. The chaplain passed around copies of the hymns and we commenced to sing. The patient sang along without any need for the sheet music. Her face was alight with joy and it was obvious she was ready to "go home." By the end of our "concert," there was not a dry eye in the house, but they were not tears of sorrow.

What a special experience this was for everyone involved. The family thanked us profusely and praised the hospital for its extraordinary service. I went away more lighthearted and saw my other patients through new eyes. I wondered if anyone else needed a song.

Edgar Martin
Looks to the
Future

by Judith Ferrell, Public Relations
Tuomey Regional Medical Center—Sumter, South Carolina

"When I was growing up, I wanted to be a doctor because I was fascinated by science and the way the human body worked. Today, I'm a science writer and now I get to do research and write articles that explain science and health to lots of people."

For Edgar Martin, it was a spring day much like any other in the South. The retired Santee Print Company employee was working in his yard and looking forward to a summer of fishing when the pain struck.

"People just have no idea how bad this hurts—this was worse than a heart attack," Martin notes. His pain was due to an aortic aneurysm which was about to rupture. The aneurysm had been discovered four years earlier, but Martin, who suffers from several chronic diseases, was too weak to undergo the necessary surgery at the time. This was unfortunate, because should the aneurysm rupture at any point, it would almost certainly kill him.

Rushed to Tuomey Regional Medical Center, Martin underwent an emergency procedure performed by vascular surgeon Dr. Christopher Carsten. But things almost didn't happen that way. At first, both Martin and his family were certain he needed to be transferred to a larger medical center for surgery.

That's where Michael Frisina, director of surgical services at Tuomey, stepped in. His concern for the family was obvious and his understanding of their fear and uncertainty helped both Martin's wife and their daughters grapple with the situation.

"I was able to explain to the family that Mr. Martin's condition was so dangerous there was a very good possibility he wouldn't survive the transfer to another facility. Also, there really was no need to move him because we had everything available here at Tuomey to perform the surgery he required," Frisina explains. It was just the assurance the family needed.

That emergency procedure saved Edgar Martin's life. Throughout his recovery, Michael Frisina kept in touch, providing reassurance, prayer and a listening ear. And though he spent nineteen days in intensive care as a result of some complications, Martin's determination to return home never wavered.

"Doctors told me they've never seen anyone recover this quickly. I was ready to go home the third day," says Martin. He couldn't be more pleased about his experience at Tuomey. "My family and I just can't say enough about everyone at the hospital—the people in surgery, the folks in the ICU, the nurses, the doctors—everybody. And, of course, Michael was around to help us get through it. Everyone was just wonderful. I wouldn't be here if it wasn't for them."

On his sixty-ninth birthday, Edgar Martin went home from

Tuomey. Thanks to the advanced surgical techniques now available here at home, he can look forward to visits by his grandchildren and playing with the Boston bull terriers his wife raises. It's a future we hope he thoroughly enjoys.

The
Lamp

by Mary Jo Sullivan, RN, BSN, MSN, Director of Heart and Vascular Nursing
St. Elizabeth Health Center—Youngstown, Ohio

"When I was growing up, I wanted to be a nun because I thought that was the best way to be close to God. Today, I am kind of like a nun because through my work of providing peace and comfort to others, I see the face of God."

One rainy Saturday afternoon, my sisters and I decided to update our dress-up wardrobe by visiting our mother's hope chest. Instead of the crocheted doilies, table linens, and the like with which young ladies readied themselves for married life, we found treasures from her youth: her eighth grade graduation gown, her first prom dress and a small white ceramic piece that looked like a genie's lamp. This caught my eye and my curiosity.

I ran to my mother, shared my discovery, and asked her why she saved a genie's lamp. Did it have magical powers like the one in the Aladdin tale? She replied that it was a keepsake used in a symbolic ceremony she experienced when she was a student nurse in 1953. The lamp symbolized the spirit of Florence Nightingale, historically known as "The Lady with the Lamp." She went on to explain that when she and her student nurse classmates completed their capping ceremony, each was presented with this symbolic lamp.

To her, the lamp symbolized hope and help for those in need. From her early childhood, she had dreamed of becoming a nurse. Unfortunately, when she reached her senior year in nursing school, her family suffered severe financial setbacks and her career dreams were put on hold. To help her family, she secured a position as a nursing assistant. Some time later, she met her husband. My father and five children later, she no longer had time to consider her own career needs.

Ironically, when I became a senior in high school, my older sister enrolled in a diploma nursing program. To meet the course requirements, she took some refresher science classes at our community college. My mother accompanied her out of curiosity. She quickly realized that her dream could still become a reality. That fall, with the support of my father and the rest of the family, she enrolled in the two-year associate degree program offered by the college. As if by second nature, I too enrolled in the associate degree program the following year and joined my mother.

1977 was a year I'll never forget: my older sister graduated from her diploma program and Mother and I graduated from our community college program and, in addition, Mother was nominated "Student Nurse of the Year-1977" for Kent State University.

This year marks our twenty-fifth year in this profession. Mother has gone on to become a certified gerontological nurse. My sister and I went on to complete our bachelor's degrees. My sister is now a nurse educator in the business she shares with her husband.

I went on to complete my masters in nursing. After twelve years in critical care, my calling was to an administrative role in nursing. I may never have known of my mother's dream or my own call to nursing had I not discovered the greatest treasure in Mother's hope chest: the lamp.

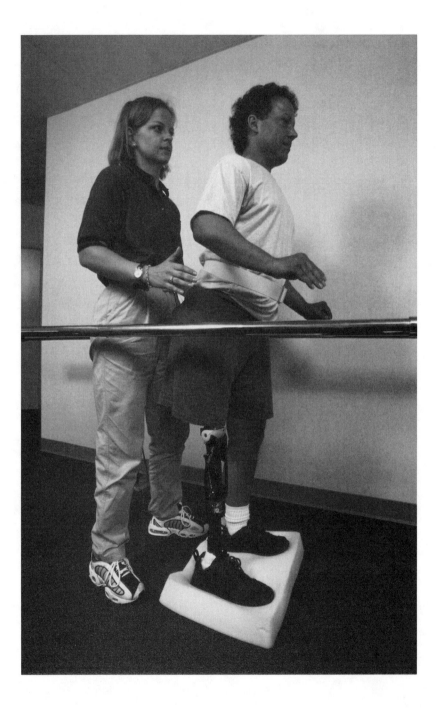

Entertaining
Angels

by Daryl Lee Berthiaume—Customer Service Department
Marquette General Hospital—Marquette, Michigan

"When I was a child, I wanted to be a lead singer because I thought it would be cool to be the 'main man' in front of the crowd. Today I am kinda like a lead singer when I preach the Gospel, except now, the 'main Man' is Jesus Christ and not myself!"

In a regional hospital like Marquette General, there are countless everyday heroes. Many daily acts of kindness go unnoticed or unrecognized. I would like to share one that is worth remembering.

First, I would like to go on record as saying that I am just a humble servant of God and not accustomed to singing my own praises. I do, however, want to share an experience when I was in a unique position to go above and beyond the usual protocol; to not only better the overall health care experience, but also to reaffirm the faith and kindness of mankind in general.

When recounting another's act of selflessness and heroism, it is difficult to capture the true essence of the individual or the act. We view the circumstances from the third-person perspective, only from the outside. When a moment is retold by a person who was involved, then you get a feel for the story from the inside. For this reason and this reason alone, I will share one of many experiences where I was able to be a beacon of light and hope. An everyday hero, of sorts.

I work in the customer service department at Marquette General Hospital (MGH), in Marquette, Michigan. I am often the first person a patient or visitor will see when they come to MGH. In my years of employment, I have had the privilege of showing many visitors to MGH what a quality, integrity-filled overall health care experience should look and feel like.

I was in such a position when in the summer of 2002, a man suffered a stroke and was transported from his hometown (over two hours away) to MGH. The stress of that event was so great that his wife suffered heart failure and also had to be admitted for triple bypass surgery. The couple's daughter, whom I shall refer to as Lily, had to fly into Michigan from Colorado to be with them and facilitate the post-release home care. When the couple had been cared for, treated, and then released, Lily took them back to their home where she stayed to care for them. After Lily and her parents had been discharged, I discovered that a key piece of luggage Lily had brought with her from Colorado had been missing when her plane arrived, only to be returned to MGH *after* Lily and her parents were back in their hometown. I received the luggage from the airport courier and upon discovering that they had already been discharged, I immediately set out to locate and contact Lily's parents' home. I called and proceeded to explain the situation and told Lily I would take care of the arrangements to safely return her bag to her that day. Lily was so moved by my generosity and willingness to help, coupled with the fact that she had been through a traumatizing ordeal, that she began to unload her emotional burden.

I listened, and after our almost half-hour conversation ended, we had bonded. She felt relief, I felt a sense of accomplishment, and we both felt that we had made a friend in the other.

Lily received her luggage that very same day. A month or two later, I received a letter of appreciation saying that her parents were living independently and doing well. It was signed—the Mayor of Littleton, Colorado.

If any of you reading this know the name of Littleton, Colorado, then you know of the terrible tragedy that occurred there. You know the senselessness from a third person point-of-view. Lily knows it from the inside, as only an elected official and leader could know it.

In the Book of Hebrews, chapter 13, verses one and two state: "Let brotherly love continue. Do not forget to entertain strangers, for by doing so, some have unwittingly entertained angels."

If there was ever a person who needed to have her faith in mankind reaffirmed, and to know that love for one another is still alive, it was Lily, the mayor of Littleton, Colorado.

I thank God and MGH for this job and for the opportunity to serve and be a hero to someone…even if it's just returning their luggage.

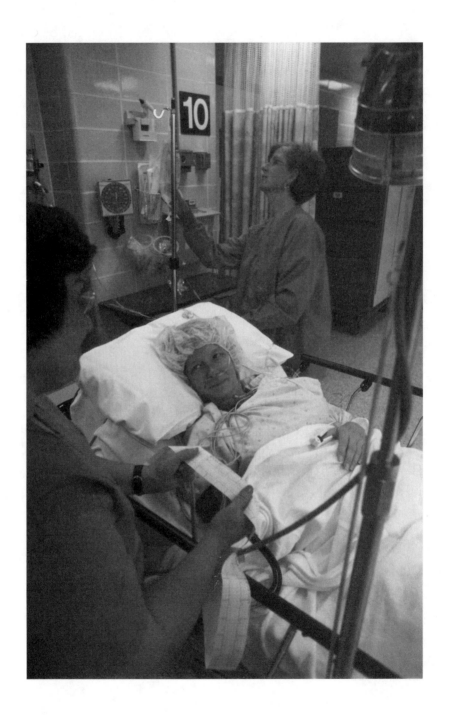

A Peek behind Woodstock's Wall

by Cassie Evans Winter, Public Relations Director
Rome Memorial Hospital—Rome, New York

"When I was growing up, I wanted to be a baseball player because Ted Williams was my hero. Today, I am kind of like a baseball player because I am part of a team working towards a common goal."—Richard Simpson

Nurses are the everyday heroes of hospitals because they give of themselves to make a difference in the lives of others every day. That commitment often extends beyond the workplace when they become volunteers in our community, like Richard Simpson, RN, CCRN, Critical Care Coordinator at Rome Memorial Hospital in Rome, New York.

Richard Simpson "worked like a dog and was exhausted at the end of each shift," but he said volunteering at Woodstock '99 was a very rewarding experience. He'd do it again tomorrow if given the chance.

Simpson is one of several Rome Memorial Hospital employees who volunteered to be part of the on-site medical team at Woodstock, which drew approximately 200,000 music fans to Rome, New York, for the July 23-25 festival in 1999. He worked the 8 a.m. shift in a medical tent across from the Emerging Artists Stage, along with a team of six or seven EMTs, a pediatric nurse from Syracuse, and a nurse and three emergency medicine physicians from Brooklyn.

The sick and injured wandered into "MASH 201" on their own two feet or were transported by golf cart at a rate of approximately 25 m.p.h. during the day shift.

"For the most part, we met nice kids who did stupid stuff. They stayed out in the sun too long and didn't drink enough water. Heat exhaustion was by far the major problem. However, we sent 98 percent of our cases back to the concert," he said.

MASH 201 saved the life of one man who went into cardiac arrest, was resuscitated, and then transported to urgent care. "We were told he survived," Simpson said. "The health department took pictures of us for the successful resuscitation."

"It was very challenging, but in many ways it was medicine and nursing the way you'd like it—all patient care and minimal paperwork. That's why it was so efficient," Simpson said.

Simpson recalled one kid who said he was nineteen, but didn't look a day over fourteen. The teen walked from the mosh pit at the main stage to Simpson's tent, which was about a quarter of a mile away.

"Suffering from heat exhaustion, he looked like a ghost, with eyes as big around as saucers," Simpson described. The teen said he got trampled in the mosh pit.

Talking a mile a minute, nonstop, the teen described how he had "borrowed" his father's car to go to Woodstock '99, just as his own father had done thirty years prior to attend the original concert in 1969. As the boy slowed to take a breath, he looked down at the IV that Simpson had started to get some fluids into him and went into a panic.

"I've got to have a doctor's note," he pleaded with Simpson. "I don't want my father to think I did anything illegal this weekend."

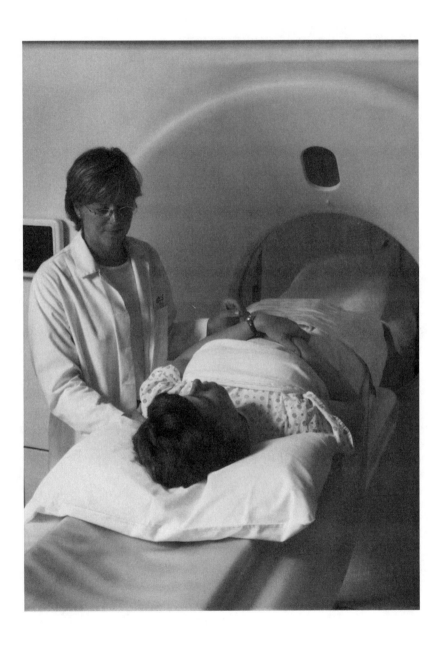

True Confessions of a Psychiatric Nurse

by Joan Strenio, RN, CS, MSN—Psych
St. Elizabeth Health Center, St. Joseph Health Center—Youngstown, Ohio

"When I was growing up, I wanted to be a florist because I liked to see plants and flowers grow, blossom and become arranged in beautiful bouquets. Today, I am like a florist because I get to witness people's lives become rearranged, grow and blossom with therapy."

I went into nursing when I was a teen
When options for women were nil, it would seem
Teaching and nursing, our choices were few
For professional jobs, "women's lib" was still new.

I was told I was good in science and math
So counselors steered me to this noble path
Where I worked as a nurse's aide for quite a few years
Finishing high school and college, my goal was now clear.

But as I studied medicine, surgery and such
I knew I really didn't like it that much
The study of the mind was where it was at
I took to psychiatry—for me, that was that!
(But if I'm honest, I confess, I'm a klutz
In all things mechanical, I am just a bust!)

So I worked on my skills in assessing the mind
And learned when to set limits and when to be kind
I now teach "Managing Illness" and cognitive skills
And how to avoid the inevitable "battle of wills."

Yes, I am a Psych Nurse, have been for years
And I've learned from experience what's abundantly clear
That patients need nurses to show them the way
To mind/body health—AND THAT'S WHY I STAY!

DThe.ecision

by Jeanne Dunn, RN, Staff Development Director
Oneida Healthcare Center—Oneida, New York

"When I was growing up, I wanted to be an interior decorator because I liked the idea of 'breathing new life' into a room and making it the best that it could be with a few inspiring color or texture updates. Today, I am kind of like an interior decorator since I try to inspire and 'breathe new life' into our nurses through education to enable them to reach their greatest potential."

"No way, Janet. I love my job," I replied. "I'm perfectly happy as a medical/surgical nurse." I had bumped into our hospital's staff development coordinator in a crowded department store.

Sadly explaining that she would not be returning from her medical leave of absence, Janet's eyes suddenly twinkled and she breathed, "Jeanne, you should apply for the staff development job!"

"I couldn't do that job," I thought to myself. "Besides, I love patient contact. I love my coworkers." While I mentally talked myself out of it, Janet was busy trying to convince me to take on the challenge of a career change. Leaning on her shopping cart, she expounded on what she thought were some of my best qualities and assured me that not only could I do it, but I could do it well. We parted, but not before she made me promise I would at least talk to our director about it.

Two days later, Alexis, Maureen and I sat in the hospital cafeteria on break. "I bumped into Janet Burton this week." I tried to sound nonchalant as I told them of Janet's efforts to encourage me to apply for the staff development position.

"Do it! Do it!" they both said in unison. They reminded me that I loved to orient new nurses to the unit and acted like a "mother hen" when inexperienced staff needed direction or extra help. "You'd be perfect for a job like that," they whispered excitedly.

Unsettled and hoping to lighten the conversation, I chuckled, "And who would decorate for holidays if I wasn't there?" I was self-proclaimed chief holiday decorator for our unit and was always the first to suggest we put the pumpkin cutouts on each patient's door or haul out the Christmas tree. I picked up my stethoscope and rose to leave. Alexis and Maureen followed along happily, assuring me all the way back to the med/surg unit that the decorating could somehow continue without me.

In the next few days, I considered all the pros and cons of changing jobs. While the possibility seemed to be ever growing, I continued my mantra, "But I love my job." I had a multitude of questions swimming in my mind. "What would be expected of me? Was I really qualified? Would I enjoy this kind of work? How would I feel about not caring for patients anymore?"

Finally, I made an appointment to see the director of nursing.

Diane was warm and encouraging. She asked me many questions and I had answers for all of them. I asked questions too, lots of them. Somehow it seemed right that I complete the job application she offered me.

I did become the hospital's new staff development director. Never had I taken such a risk, leaving a position that I loved dearly after fourteen years. But as time passed, I came to realize that the change had been the greatest blessing in my career as a nurse. Instead of caring for patients, I began to care for nurses. Instead of guiding patients on their journeys to the bathroom, I was guiding nurses to new levels of knowledge and skill. In my new role, I was indirectly improving patients' care by supporting the caregivers.

Nurses care not only for patients, but for one another. They are healers of the soul as well as the body. Janet, Diane and my coworkers from the med/surg unit helped to heal the raw spot of fear and uncertainty that had surfaced in my soul. They gave me the support and encouragement I needed to make the change.

The first day of my new job, I nervously unlocked the door to the staff development office. I snapped on the lights and, to my delight, plastered there on every wall were holiday decorations of every kind: Easter, Halloween, Christmas, Valentine's Day. Amidst the color display was a poster that read, "Good Luck, Jeanne, our new staff development coordinator." It was signed by all the nurses on the med/surg unit. And there on the empty desk sat a lush dish garden with a welcome note from Diane. As I sat down at the desk, Janet's words of support and urging hung in the air. These everyday heroes had all rallied behind me and encouraged me to walk forward in faith and meet the challenge of stepping out of my comfort zone.

I breathed a happy sigh as I settled in and thought, "I love my job."

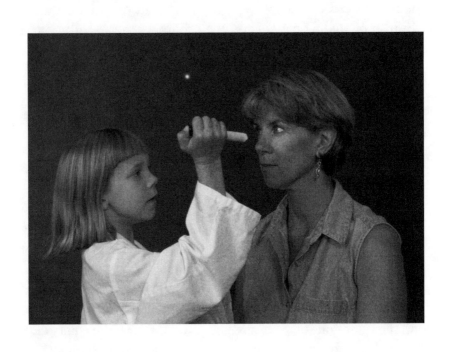

Touching
Hearts

by Barbara A. Scales, RN, CCRN, CAPA, RM, Nurse Orientor
Harrison Center Outpatient Surgery—Syracuse, New York

"When I was growing up, I wanted to be a nurse because of two very special women. Our neighbor, Mrs. McGowan, responded to a deadly car crash up the road from where we lived. She sat and held the hand of a mother dying on the scene. Although our home was about one mile away, I could hear that woman screaming. At the early age of four, I realized that what she did that night took courage and compassion. The other woman is my Aunt Barbara, who has been a nurse for many years. She rarely talks to me about her experiences, but there is something special in her eyes. In her eyes is an unspoken answer for why nurses do what they do. May God bless them both."

When catastrophe strikes, nurses doing triage never ask, "Should I get involved?" They just step in and get the job done. But what about triaging ourselves?

Our small outpatient surgery center has been inundated with tragic events this past year, leaving not a single person untouched either by personal experience or by sharing a coworker's grief. Names do not matter, for they are all part of our family. Although my teammates may not realize it, they are part of the reason why we get out of bed every day.

When one nurse's husband's income was decreased, some co-workers created a donation box for food to refill the family's pantry cupboards until her husband could get his feet back on the ground.

Last Christmas, our directors decided that instead of accepting gifts from the employees, that it was more in the spirit of the season to give any money collected in the form of small donations to the needy, which included one of our medical records support team. Through no fault of her own, this woman was struggling just to feed her family, never mind buy her children gifts for under the tree.

One nurse's sister was diagnosed with vulvular cancer. Each privately shuddered, "My God, what if that was me?" Somehow this brave warrior smiled through the tears. Since her sister couldn't have children, she had become a foster parent, so our coworker was frequently at her sister's house to change dressings, help potty the toddler, make meals or run errands. She nurtured her sister back to health with the assistance of her "family at work" lending a tissue to cry into, staying late to cover her shift, or pitching in to finish her assignment to get her out on time.

The hardest story to tell is the death of our operating room nurse manager's son. It must have seemed like an endless agony to her, but those of us on the outside looking in felt as though it happened in the blink of an eye. No one expects illness to rob our youth, but leukemia is a frightful adversary. One afternoon he was too tired to go to wrestling practice. Within a week he was on a ventilator fighting for his life. His loss took the wind out of all our sails. A senior OR staff member stepped up to the helm and guided her cohorts through this murky time, managing it with grace. I watched in awe as her group of coworkers tethered their love together and buoyed their grieving manager in their arms safely onto the other shore.

After unsuccessful years of fertility testing and in-vitro implantations, our newest member had conceived without outside intervention! We were thrilled for her and her husband. Their dream had finally come true, but the dream was short-lived. Her doctor used the term "blighted ovum." Trying to "pass" the products of conception she nearly hemorrhaged to death. She tried to come back to work after four days. It was obvious she was not capable of working so her "working family" sent her home with strict instructions to go to bed and stay there. A week later she came back a little pale, but willing and that's when she rescued me.

My nineteen-year-old daughter redeveloped sub-pleural effusions of undiagnosed etiology, causing her a great deal of pain and extreme fatigue. For three weeks, we watched and waited, going through test after test. It was emotionally exhausting. After ten different doctors had rendered their opinions, it was believed to be an autoimmune disorder, not a virus. One afternoon while at work, my daughter called me in excruciating pain and crying for help. Torn with completing my assignment and the need to be at my daughter's side, I became sullen and withdrawn. This new coworker picked up on it immediately. I held myself together until she gave me a hug and I could sense her loss through my own grief. It was as if our two hearts felt and shared the other's burden, and I broke down into sobs. My focus on work was shattered. When I approached my nurse manager for permission to leave, I didn't have to say a word. She gave me permission to leave, but more importantly, she gave me permission to be a mom before being a nurse. That's what helped me through that day; she understood.

Nurses have a "working family" to lean on when the going gets tough. And sometimes nurses need reminding that we are human too, and it's okay not to be okay.

A New Meaning for Physical Education

by April J. Lombardo, RN, C MBA CDE, Nurse Educator
Morgantown, West Virginia

"When I was growing up, I wanted to be a physical education teacher because I was really athletic and enjoyed playing sports. Today, I'm kind of like a phys ed teacher because I teach a wide audience about physical illnesses."

The job nurse educator? It has its downfalls. For example, sometimes I think my phone number is the only one the hospital operators know, but like most other nurses, I come to work to meet my own inner needs. There's a certain magnetism about nursing. Amidst the frustration are shining stars (beaming faces) that keep me coming back. Let me tell you about one such face.

Not too long ago, as I lamented over my "things to do" list, Mrs. D. showed up at my office door. One of the step-down-unit nurses had pointed her my way.

"Hi," I said with surprise, pleased to see one of my former patients.

She looked so terrific in her soft pink sweater with carefully chosen earrings and necklace to match. She was so "put together" I'm sure she took extra time to dress on this morning. Her eyes were bright; yet there was an unmistakable serenity about her this day.

"Are you visiting someone?" I asked.

"No, I came to see you!" was her reply.

I invited her in to sit down. Without hesitation, she started to tell me how it was me who convinced her to do something she never thought she could. I recall the anxiety that emanated from her hospital bed: her wild eyes, tense muscles, and short attention span. I recall her holding up her hands in front of her face as if to guard herself from the insulin syringe I held out for her to see. But most of all, I recall the tears, joy and sense of accomplishment and the grateful, warm embrace I received following her very first self-injection.

After she left my office, I realized she came to honor me. She had asked her husband to take time out of his busy, chore-laden day to drive her to the hospital just to see me. And he did. And he waited outside on the stone bench until she had completed what she came to do. On this particular day, seemingly all rote and redundancy, one sweet little lady reminded me that I make a difference—and that feels good.

Are You Feeling Important?

by Georgette L. Doty, RN, BSN—Performance Improvement
St. Joseph Health Center—Warren, Ohio

"When I was growing up, I wanted to be a teacher because I was excited and energized by learning new things—I wanted to be able to pass that excitement and energy along to others. Today, as a nurse, I am also a teacher because I am able to share my knowledge and expertise with patients, families, coworkers and other members of the health care team. It still energizes and excites me to be able to do that!"

Judging from the title of this little story, you may just want to pass it by... not another story about nurses feeling unappreciated and unimportant. But bear with me, dear reader—I promise that by the end of my story you will be chuckling and possibly wiping away tears of laughter from your eyes.

Prior to working for Humility of Mary Health Partners, I was a manager of a large, freestanding chronic hemodialysis unit. One of the first things I did each morning was gather the treatment flowsheets from the day before. I would review each patient's flowsheet, looking for anything out of the ordinary that may have occurred during the dialysis treatment.

I also reviewed any documentation on the flowsheets for content and appropriateness. There were several disciplines that documented, including social workers, dietitians, nurses and patient care technicians. Sometimes, though the occasions were usually few and far between, staff had to be reminded to include things that had occurred during the treatment.

One morning, as I was completing my flowsheet audit, I came across a bizarre statement that was documented by one of the RNs. The statement was in quotation marks and was obviously a direct statement from the patient. It made no sense to me, so I asked the RN who had recorded this to explain what she had written. The documentation went something like, "The patient states, 'I think this medication is making me feel important'."

When the RN reread her notes, she couldn't stop laughing. Seeing her laugh, with tears running down her cheeks, made me laugh. Every time she attempted to explain the documentation to me, she laughed even harder. Before long, we were both reaching for tissues to wipe off the mascara that was running down our faces.

What was she trying to say? The patient she had cared for the day before was a young, vital male. He was a relatively healthy patient and was very knowledgeable about his renal disease and took an active role in his treatment. The RN had been doing medication rounds and was preparing to give the patent an EPO injection (EPO is a synthetic form of erythropoietin, a hormone manufactured in the kidney that helps the bone marrow make new red blood cells).

The patient refused the EPO and the RN explored this refusal with him a bit —he had never refused before and she was concerned. He stated that he had been having some problems in the "bedroom" and that he felt the EPO injections were making him impotent. However, when the time came to document this, the word impotent was transcribed as important!

Maybe you had to have been there, but I can honestly say that it was one of the funniest moments I have ever experienced at work. And, as nurses, we know that those moments are few and far between. I'm happy to tell you that our patient did not refuse any more EPO injections and went on to receive a very successful kidney transplant. I hope that he knows how "important" he was to all of us who cared for him.

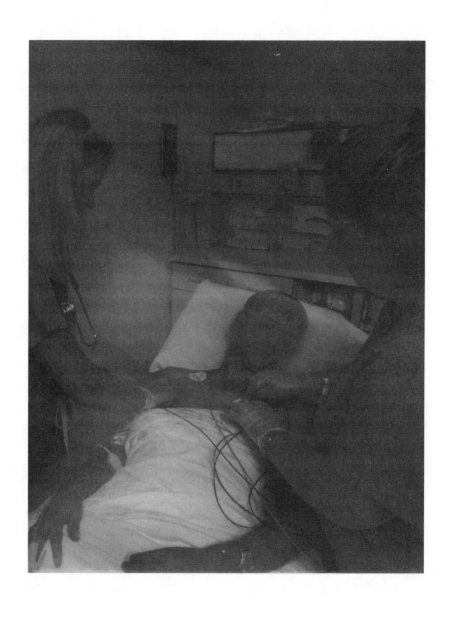

Laughter— Good for the Heart

by Debby Petuch-Stubbs, RN, BSN, Clinical Educator, Heart and Vascular Services
St. Elizabeth Health Center—Youngstown, Ohio

"When I was growing up, I wanted to be an astronomer because my attraction to the idea of experiencing something inconceivable was overwhelming. Today I am like an astronomer because, through nursing, I encounter new and fascinating situations every day."

Believe it or not, some of my most comical moments in nursing have occurred in the cardiac stress lab. The older patients had such a great sense of humor. One that comes readily to mind was a little lady who wore bilateral prosthetic legs. She had come in for a pharmacological stress test, but needed her nuclear images taken first. We got her settled on the scanner, legs and all. When the scan was completed, we helped her to a sitting position and were ready to get her back on her feet. With one of us on each side, we slid her off the table and had her upright. Suddenly, she started to giggle. She was laughing so hard that all she could do was point to her feet. We looked down to see what the problem was. This definitely was a real predicament. Her feet were both pointed backwards! Somehow, during our "getting her settled" maneuvers, we managed to spin her legs all the way around. She certainly lightened a potentially embarrassing situation.

A gentleman came to us late in the day. Another nurse and I were trying to finish up a terribly busy shift. I had this little fellow all hooked up and ready to walk on the treadmill. As he was standing in anticipation of his test, he suddenly sneezed. His dentures came flying out of his mouth, landed on the floor, and proceeded to skid toward the door.

Just then, the other RN came walking into the room and the teeth stopped at the toe of her shoe. It was as if "Jaws" had come to St. E's. The three of us laughed so hard that we had to let him rest before he could start his test. This incident made the whole dreadful day worth it (and, remarkably, there was not one chip out of the dentures!).

Last, but not least, was the ninety-two-year-old gentleman who walked for five minutes on the treadmill. If you have ever had a stress test, you can imagine the energy to do this at his age. He was very excited to get this over with because his square dancing club was meeting at noon and he couldn't be late. He didn't want to disappoint the ladies, because "at my age, I have the pick of the litter. All the other guys are dead!" They say that laughter is good for the soul, but after my years in the cardiac stress lab, I'm fairly certain it's good for the heart too!

Everyday Heroes of the Born Too Soon

by Cecelia Hughes, Executive Assistant
Navapache Regional Medical Center—Show Low, Arizona

"When I was growing up in the 1940s following World War II, I wanted to be a nurse because I enjoyed bandaging the 'wounded soldiers' when we played 'war.' Later, I added the option of also being a missionary. Today, as the wife of a retired minister, I enjoy being an executive assistant in the administration department of our regional hospital."

Every day, unseen by the population at large, nurses in neonatal intensive care units across the country care for infants born too soon. As the preemies struggle to live outside their mothers' wombs, the caregiver tends to the many needs of the newborns until the patients are well enough to be discharged weeks or months later. These caregivers are not usually celebrated in songs or stories, but they are heroes to the people whose lives they touch. This is the story of one nurse and the infant entrusted to her care.

Born on March 14, 1987, in Farmington, New Mexico, after only 24-1/2 weeks of gestation, Skylar Hughes weighed only 1 pound, 12 ounces. At 9:30 a.m., while the baby's father scrubbed with the surgical team, the attending physician cautioned, "The chances of this little baby's survival are slim to none. He's just too young."

Following the cesarean birth, the premature infant looked lifeless. His tiny body was dark blue-gray and there was no movement in his chest. The team went into action—first priority, getting oxygen into the newborn's underdeveloped lungs. On an Apgar scale of 1 to 10 (10 being a healthy baby), Skylar was rated only 1. At 4 p.m., he was considered stable, "a keeper," and was transported to Bernalillo County Medical Center in Albuquerque, New Mexico.

"For He shall give His angels charge over thee, to keep thee in all thy ways." Skylar was only one day old when these words from Psalm 91 were read over his isolette in the intensive care unit. One of the "angels" in Skylar's life-and-death struggle would be his primary nurse. As a health care professional, she knew too well the rollercoaster ride Skylar and his young parents, David and Suzette, would experience in the months to follow.

The honeymoon period started with mild lung disease and jaundice. As the baby's translucent skin broke down, liquid oozed from the cracks. Oxygen started at 20-30% was steadily elevated to 60-80%. One by one, problems developed and were treated: an open-heart valve, chronic lung disease, and a grade 3 intraventricular hemorrhage, commonly called a brain bleed.

On April 15, Skylar developed severe pneumonia. Pavalon was

ordered to paralyze his body so he would not fight the ventilator. Doctors inserted three tubes into the infant's chest, but after four days on 100 percent oxygen, it looked as if the baby would not survive. With heavy hearts, David and Suzette agreed to allow Skylar to gradually be taken off the ventilator. "There's nothing more we can do for your little boy," the doctor said. "We're going to have to leave it between him and a higher power."

Skylar's nurse had bonded with her tiny charge. She was in New York when her husband called and relayed the message that Skylar was not doing well, that "DNR" (do not resuscitate) had been ordered. She quickly cut her trip short and returned to Albuquerque.

On the Tuesday after Easter, David received a call, "Mr. Hughes, I'm glad I reached you. No one knows how to explain this, but your son is okay. We normally only take one chest tube out at a time, but we took all three tubes out and he is back to normal settings on his oxygen and vent settings. You wouldn't believe it. He's like a different baby!"

The remarkable turn of events had started Easter Sunday. Telephone wires sent the message to others: "The baby lives!"

The ride was not over, however. The fragile infant contracted pneumonia one more time and also had emergency double hernia surgery. Fortunately, a CT scan on June 18 indicated there were no brain problems.

When Skylar was finally released to go home at the end of July, his nurse said, "...to see him [Skylar] totally normal, healthy, without any brain damage, that is a miracle, and I want you to remind him every day."

It was celebration time. The city of Farmington officially welcomed Skylar home by way of newspaper, radio and television, and the couple's church declared a special Skylar Hughes Day. In their presentations at Skylar's dedication service, David and

Suzette acknowledged Skylar's nurse's contribution to their son's recovery. To them, she was a hero.

Today, at age fifteen, Skylar is 5' 10" and still growing. He is legally blind in one eye, but you would never know because he has learned to compensate with the perfect vision in his other eye. He is a happy teenager who loves to ski and play the bass guitar and drums.

A Difference to One

by Stephnie Darby, RN—Palliative Care Coordinator
St. Elizabeth Health Center—Youngstown, Ohio

"I became a nurse because I wanted to make a difference in the world. I remain in nursing with the realization that I may not be able to impact the whole world, but to those families and patients I meet, I can make a difference."

It was going to be a great shift! I was assigned a "stable" open-heart surgery patient who was more than twelve hours post-op and extubated. My second patient was a forty-nine-year old with chest pain coming to me from the cath lab. He had an NTG drip and had been pain-free since his procedure.

About two hours after his admission, he began having chest pain. His EKG showed the anticipated changes, and I began titrating his NTG drip and monitoring his vital signs closely. Because he was so unstable, I did not leave his bedside. The surgeon arrived and explained to my patient that he needed immediate surgery. As I prepared him for surgery, giving the necessary medications and filling out the proper paperwork, I looked at the frightened look on his face.

Earlier in the shift, we had chatted about his life. He told me he was a truck driver. He loved his job because he was able to see so much of the United States. He often felt regret for not being able to be at home much with his wife while they were raising their children. He was very proud of his sons and the men they had become. We had contacted his wife and she was on her way in from the East Coast.

As his vital signs further declined, he stayed amazingly lucid. I had completed all of the physical preparations for surgery, but the terrified look on his face told me that he still wasn't prepared. I put his hand in mine and asked him if I could pray with him. Together we prayed the Lord's Prayer. Those were the last words he ever spoke.

I escorted him to surgery at a full trot and he continued to deteriorate. I received the news soon afterward that he had died in surgery and I was saddened by the fact that he didn't get to tell his family goodbye. The chaplain came to the unit to talk with me before meeting the wife. I was able to share our earlier conversation which I hope brought them a sense of peace. I personally was pleased that I was able to bring him some comfort in his last moments on this earth.

I made a difference to that one person. I became a nurse because I wanted to make a difference in the world. I remain in nursing with the realization that I may not be able to impact the whole world, but to those families and patients I meet, I can make a difference.

Lessons
from a
Cowboy

by Kathleen M. Pust, RN
Sidney Health Center—Sidney, Montana

"When I was growing up, I wanted to be a nurse because I admired the women who cared for me in the hospital while I was recovering from rheumatic fever. Today, I am a hospice nurse and I am privileged to care for patients and families who are dealing with terminal illness, anticipatory grieving and death. I am blessed with the opportunity to give my patients love, care and support during their last journey of life."

Every story has a spin imparted by the magic in our minds that makes our memories come alive. In these memories live the heroes in my life, bringing me humor and great wonder at the cycle of life.

The moment of death is much the same for all of us. Suddenly, the breath of life within us is gone and we are no longer in physical communication with those we love. I have felt that breath of life leave many while at their bedside as a hospice nurse. Without a doubt, the loss of something whole and sacred like a life is a loss keenly felt by all. We honor these souls by telling their story.

I live in a rural area of Eastern Montana where men are not especially given to emotion, but instead are filled with an extra measure of independence and certainty of who they are and where they have come from. No greater example of this can be seen than in the cowboy spirit of our old-timers.

Let me introduce you to one of those cowboys. Our first encounter happened on his ranch. It took me almost an hour to find his home, driving over a rutted lane that veered off the main road and wound through a seemingly endless stretch of pasture filled with cow pies and entrenched cow paths. I crested a hill to view an old barn. There was only one vehicle path visible and it ran through the corral to a small building my mind wouldn't let me believe was his home.

After knocking on the warped and unpainted door of the house, I entered a tiny kitchen with a wood stove from which came a wonderful aroma of baking bread. I was asked to sit at a small table and as I sat down I looked up to see a picture of the president framed and hanging on the wall. It was cut from a magazine cover. The living room had a large, thick rug, and I realized after looking closely that it covered a bare earthen floor.

This dear man and his wife were the happiest people I had met that day and from within them, a peace and certainty about life flowed. He was losing weight and fighting for breath as he told me that his body was slowly giving out. He didn't ask me for a quick fix, but he did voice clearly his wish to never leave this ranch. He looked out the small window by the table into the hills and, with a wistful twist to his mouth, talked about life in this bit of wilderness. How quickly in my course of visits I learned to love his honesty, character, and love for the land and his lifestyle.

It was with awe and great sadness that I learned about his death. No, I wasn't there, but I knew his death had fulfilled his wishes. It was there, beside the little house on top of that corral hill, that he breathed his last breath of prairie air. Later, as I offered my condolences to his wife, her response was to shrug her shoulders and voice quiet acceptance of things she couldn't change.

I think of that special couple often when I see the harried, busy lives we all lead today and realize that the gift of serenity, contentment and personal identity was never a struggle for them. The house remains unoccupied since the Mrs. moved to town. Soon it will soon be a tumbling-down, weather-beaten shack: a shack that had once been a warm home filled with love and peace in the middle of nowhere.

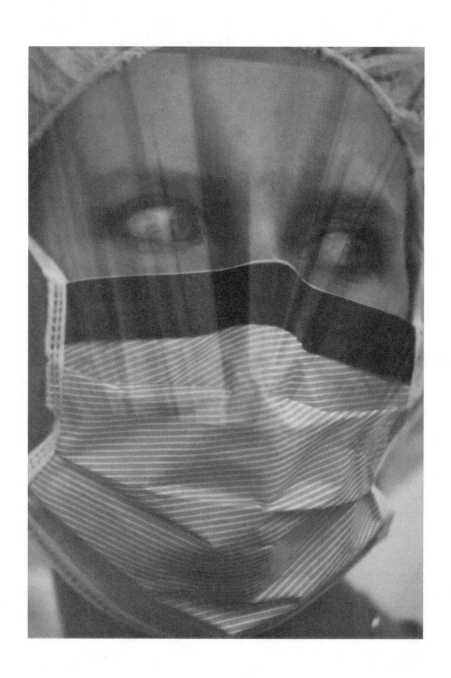

A Tale of One Angel

by Sherry Anderson, RN, BSN, CNOR, Clinical Educator-Surgical Services
St. Elizabeth Health Center—Youngstown, Ohio

"Nursing is ever-changing. There are always new and exciting procedures, products and equipment to serve our patients better. It is a humbling career in which patients put their lives in our hands and trust that we will take care of them, bringing them physical, emotional and spiritual comfort."

When I was fifteen, I had the opportunity to work at St. Elizabeth Hospital as a Red Cross volunteer. At that time, the sisters had a visible and awesome presence. I was amazed and intrigued by their gentle, caring and soft manner, as they walked down the hall in their long white habits.

I graduated in the 1960s. The only career choices for women seemed to be secretary, nurse, hairdresser, nun (if you were

Catholic), or you got married. After graduation, I enrolled at the Choffin School of Practical Nursing. During one of the clinicals, there was a brief rotation to the operating room. I loved every minute of it. When I graduated, there was nowhere else that I wanted to work but St. Elizabeth's. During my interview with Sister Mary Carl, I stated how I loved surgery and, to my good fortune, there were several openings.

After nineteen years of being a scrub nurse, I enrolled at the St. Elizabeth School of Nursing. Upon graduation, I worked on the medical/surgical floor for a year. Working in both of these areas opened my eyes to the wonders of this profession. In surgery, the nurse shares a special experience with a patient at a time of great stress. The role of the nurse is to be the patient's advocate, making certain he or she is in a safe and aseptic environment. On the med/surg unit, I experienced daily interactions with my patients and their families. Besides the direct nursing care itself, there were so many nursing functions to perform: teaching, promoting preventative medicine, and taking part in the patient's rehabilitation.

Nursing is ever-changing. There are always new and exciting procedures, products and equipment to serve our patients better. It is a humbling career in which patients put their lives in our hands and trust that we will take care of them, bringing them physical, emotional and spiritual comfort. In his/her mind, a nurse is always haunted by the question, "Have I done everything possible for this patient?"

Big City Hospital with a Small Town Philosophy

by Sarah Soden, Public Relations Specialist
Robert Packer Hospital—Sayre, Pennsylvania

"When I was growing up, I wanted to be a writer because writing helps people understand ideas, information and different points of view. Today, I am a writer and I help people understand the things they need to know."

Cara Ferber, a college student involved in a serious head-on car accident, spent three weeks in the Robert Packer Hospital Intensive Care Unit in March 2002. Her recovery was uncertain due to the seriousness of her multiple injuries, but thanks to the efforts of the entire trauma team, Cara continues to make a remarkable recovery. On her birthday (August 20), Cara and her parents, Jack Ferber and Deborah Sattler of New Jersey, explained how much the care their daughter received at RPH meant to their whole family:

"One evening in late March, we received a phone call from a Tompkins County sheriff saying that our daughter had been in a serious accident and was being brought to Robert Packer Hospital. We got right in the car and drove here, and found ourselves in a small town with this big medical center. We were initially skeptical of a small town hospital, but we were so grateful to find such incredible competency there. This was a 'big city' hospital with a 'small town' philosophy which we found ideal. When we learned how critical her situation was, we realized we would be here for a while.

"It was amazing how the staff helped us take care of everything. Clinical coordinator Kay Daniels had a room for us across the street in the Patterson Building and even got us a charger for our cell phone—the staff really took care of Cara and us. Nurses even came in on their days off to see how Cara was. The care she received could not be duplicated anywhere. Words seem inadequate—all we can say is thank you so much for giving us our child back. You are all angels."

Cara continues her rehabilitation on an outpatient basis and the RPH trauma team celebrates her recovery!

Guardian
Angels

by Diane Kupensky, RN, MSN, CNS
St. Elizabeth Health Center—Youngstown, Ohio

"When I was growing up, I always wanted to be a nurse because I had the 'disease to please,' whether it was pleasing the human species or animals. Caring for others seems like a gift and an honor to me, so a career in nursing seemed a perfect fit—an ideal way to put my seemingly incurable 'disease' to good use. Today, I am like a 'facilitator' of others' pain, emotions and physical needs because I feel that is my life's purpose. I love being a nurse."

I tried to remember why I wanted to become a nurse, but do not remember any revelations or "lightning bolt" moments that inspired me. I just remember *always* wanting to be a nurse. It was just a part of who I am. Oprah Winfrey talks about "the disease to please" and I think that this affliction hit me early on as a child. Whether it was taking care of dolls, pets or brothers and sisters, it just came naturally to me. It seemed like I was always the one to run for the box of Band-Aids and willing to clean off everyone's scrapes and cuts. Maybe it was a sense of "taking care of things." It was, and still is, an honor to take care of people, especially those who open their hearts and souls to us nurses....

One story that I tell at family get-togethers (with some pride, I might add) is about when my own father shared with me some personal, intimate details of an out-of-body experience he had after suffering a major heart attack. Being a very stoic, strict disciplinarian, my father never shared any feelings with any of us. I never expected him to divulge any private experiences, especially to me, the youngest of six children. However, one day he asked to speak to me "because I was a nurse." He started telling me about being in the ER while they were doing CPR on him. He felt like he was floating up in the corner of the room. He remembered all the conversations of the nurses in the room. He experienced the feeling of falling toward a white light and being pulled back only to have excruciating chest pain after the successful CPR. He felt very angry that he had been brought back to a world of pain from the peaceful "other side." He told me never to fear dying because it is a beautiful and peaceful experience. He shared his experience with me because I was a nurse. In a family of scientists, physicists and mathematicians, he chose me because I would not try to analyze or dissect the experience or try to prove or disprove that it happened. I just listened, non-judgmentally, not questioning any aspect of its truth. That was one of the most cherished moments of my nursing career.

I've experienced other, similar moments that were equally touching in the last twenty-five years. Even though it may not be considered "savvy" to have the "disease to please," I consider it a wonderful gift. I feel that I get more back, much more, than I am giving. I'm proud to say I'm a nurse!

Scrooge

by Nick Adams, Communications Writer
Wellmont Health System—Kingsport, Tennessee

"**W**hen I was growing up, I wanted to be a cowboy because I loved the idea of strapping on my guns, shooting it out and saving the day. Today, I am kind of like a cowboy because I face daily challenges and my job is to help others with their problems."—*Eric Deaton*

"Ebenezer Scrooge wasn't a bad manager."

This is not something one would expect to hear from a man recently chosen to receive the Health Care Heroes Cup of Kindness Meritorious Service Award, an honor annually given to the area's top hospital administrator by a local business magazine. To those who know Eric Deaton, vice president of finance/operations at Wellmont Bristol Regional Medical Center in Bristol, Tennessee, the statement seems even more unlikely.

"Scrooge made money," Deaton continued. "He ran an efficient business that turned a consistent profit. But with Scrooge, there was something missing."

And that missing something—empathy for all people, coworkers and customers alike—is what sets Deaton apart from the classic Dickens character and many in the business field today.

"I'm really not that much of a numbers-cruncher," Deaton said. "I'm much more of a people person."

That was evidenced one Christmas when the aforementioned Ebenezer Scrooge was the topic of a manager's meeting at WBRMC. Deaton treated his group to a screening of the 1938 movie version of A Christmas Carol before discussing the management applications of the story.

"We talked about the good and bad parts of Scrooge's management style," Deaton said. "Yeah, he made money, but there's giving and caring and putting yourself in the place of others—all of those things make a good manager, too."

Not that Deaton isn't concerned with the mathematical aspects of his job description—he is responsible for analyzing all hospital costs, expenses, revenues and reimbursements. In fact, Deaton has excelled at his post, turning what was a $6 million operating loss to a $1.3 million gain in the two years he's worked at WBRMC.

"And we've turned things around without affecting the quality of patient care," Deaton said. "We've basically worked on doing things more efficiently."

Deaton also credits his managers at the hospital for their input and cooperation in moving the ledgers from the red to the black.

"I've got a great group. My managers are awesome people to work with," he said. "I was nominated for this award by those managers and I can't think of a better compliment than to get such recognition from the people you work with."

It's easy to see why Deaton has had a big impact on his staff. Like any good leader, Deaton leads by example.

During the hospital's fund-raising campaign for the American Cancer Society Relay for Life one year, Deaton—a young man with a full head of hair—shaved his head to foster awareness of the disease and its effects.

"It was easy to do," Deaton said. "My mother passed away in 2000 from cancer, and one of the more traumatic aspects of the ordeal for her and my father was the loss of her hair due to the chemotherapy treatments. It (shaving my head) gave me a chance to raise some money and to honor the people like my mom who have had to go through all that."

Despite a job that requires a great deal of his time, Deaton is also active in the community. He is a member of the Milligan College Executive Council, the East Tennessee State University Pirate Club Board of Directors, the Johnson City Chamber of Commerce Governmental Relations Committee and Community Health Committee, the United Way of Johnson City Board of Directors and the United Emmaus Community. He is also chairman of the Munsey United Methodist Church Parish Nurse Program.

Because he has very little free time, Deaton said it is important to love what you do.

"We're in a very serious business—taking care of people. We need to take it seriously," he said. "We have demanding work, and we have to spend a lot of time away from our families, so it's important that we like what we do."

"My job is like a big puzzle every day—trying to get all the pieces to fit together to keep the hospital financially viable. It's a constant challenge, and that's what I love."

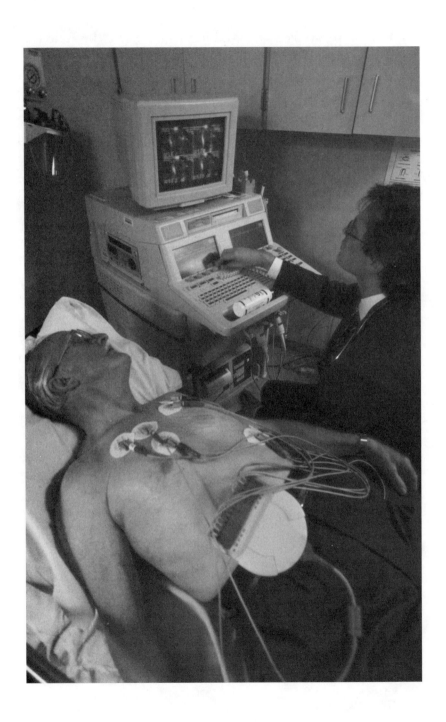

Why I Chose Nursing as a Career and Working in Long-Term Care

by Holly Malone, RN—Humility House
Humility House—Austintown, Ohio

"When I was growing up, I wanted to be a nurse because as a candy striper I loved the environment of the hospital and helping people. Today, I'm like a subway in New York, running twenty-four hours a day being a wife, mother, grandmother, sister and friend, and working full time."

I learned at an early age that there are three ingredients of happiness: faith, hope and love.

Faith—to believe in God: a trust that does not rest on logical proof or material evidence, "faith in miracles."

Hope—to look forward with confidence of fulfillment.

Love—an intense, affectionate concern for other people.

As I thought about a career, nursing came to mind. I could be with people and help them by giving them hope for the future. Since I would be practicing the three ingredients everyday, I would be happy.

I worked in a hospital for two years. I was pleased to see the patients recuperate quickly, but saddened because I kept losing new friends. I decided to try long-term care. I loved the continuity of my patients here and felt that I could give better care because I knew everything about them. I was able to sense any change in their condition much more quickly.

I continue to use the three ingredients of happiness in my long-term care career and I am truly happy.

My Inspirational
Angel

by Anna Marie Ottney, RN, BSN, CCTC, Transplant Coordinator
St. Elizabeth Health Center—Youngstown, Ohio

"When work gets tough and I wonder what I am doing here, I think of my cousin and the inspiration he gave me to become a nurse."

After high school, I went straight to nursing school and started working at St. Elizabeth's in 1982. In 1988, when it was announced that we would be doing transplants here at our hospital, I was very excited. I knew then that I had to be involved with the transplant program. As a transplant nurse, I have always used my cousin as an example of what transplant patients can achieve.

I knew that I wanted to be a nurse as a sophomore in high school. It was during this time that my cousin, Richard, went into renal failure and needed a kidney transplant. He eventually received his transplant, but had a long hospitalization and numerous complications. My knowledge of nursing and medicine was minimal at this point in my life, but I remember being fascinated and touched by the stories my aunt told me about the wonderful nurses who took care of my cousin during his long ordeal.

Richard eventually recovered, went to college, got married and had four beautiful children. His transplant lasted twenty years. In 1998, Richard died due to complications from hepatitis. When work gets tough and I wonder what I am doing here, I think of my cousin and the inspiration he gave me to become a nurse. I believe that he never would have had twenty great years after his transplant were it not for the competent and caring nurses who cared for him during every inpatient and outpatient visit. Richard will always be the angel that inspires me to continue working as a nurse.

Not Just Another Day at the Office

by Sarah Soden, Public Relations Specialist
Robert Packer Hospital—Sayre, Pennsylvania

Sometimes a day at the office is not just another day. On a fall day in 2002, a patient arrived at the registration desk at Guthrie's Big Flats, New York, regional office, confused and agitated. He was unable to provide any information to float receptionist Elaine Ellers and was having difficulty speaking as well as problems writing when asked to fill out forms. He had no identification with him.

Medical office assistant Judy Mills overheard the difficulties and came out to assist. She discovered that the patient had been dropped off by a friend who had subsequently left. At this point, the patient exited the building. Fearing for his safety if he wandered around outside, Mills sat with him on a bench outside the office waiting for the friend's return. Sharon Nugent, LPN, along with Dr. Madhu Jain, went outside to see if they recognized the patient or could help in some other way. Dr. Jain attempted to help the man remember his name or any other personal information and Mills continued to encourage the patient as well, asking simple "yes" or "no" questions in hopes of learning his name or other identifying facts.

The patient was increasingly frustrated with himself, but was continually reassured by staff that they would spend whatever time was necessary to help him. At this time, the patient began to march around the parking lot and would not return to the building. He was staggering and very unsteady on his feet; Mills walked with him to prevent him from falling. The patient ended up sitting on the curb and Mills sat with him, speaking to him and trying to help him relax.

Sherry Stanbro and Denise Parrotte, LPN, came out to see if they recognized the patient. Parrotte thought he was a patient of Dr. Jan Goossens, which Deb Holley, LPN, confirmed, so Dr. Goossens was summoned to speak with the patient. While this breakthrough was taking place, however, the patient began to walk across the medical building's yard toward a nearby hotel. Disoriented and somewhat combative, he continued toward the road with Mills and Holley close behind, talking to him and preventing him from walking into traffic despite his struggle to break free. At this point, Dr. Goossens arrived on the scene, recognized the man as his patient, and was able to get the patient to speak with him. The patient was very comfortable with Dr. Goossens and returned willingly to the office with him to be examined.

The whole event lasted more than an hour, but the patient was kept safe and not allowed to wander alone in his disoriented state. A few days later, he was admitted to the hospital with a brain tumor, the unfortunate cause of his agitation and disorientation.

Angels Among Us: With God All Things Are Possible

by Cassantra Clinkscale, RN, Surgery
St. Elizabeth Health Center—Youngstown, Ohio

"When I was growing up, I wanted to be a nurse because nursing seemed to be the only profession that took care of suffering humanity. Today, I am a nurse because I was chosen by God. He granted me my heart's desire."

As I leaned back and began to meditate on the questions of why I became a nurse and why I stayed in nursing, my mind went back many years, approximately fifty-two, when my heart's desire was to be a nurse. "I had a dream." As a young child, I remember playing nurse with my friends and my sisters and brothers. I was the oldest of nine children, so I had plenty of patients (smile). At Christmastime, Santa would bring me a nurse's kit. I had little plastic thermometers, needles, stethoscopes, a nurse's cap and candy pills for medicine. It was lots of fun. Even though it was my desire, the reality of becoming a nurse was slim to none.

I graduated from high school in 1961 at the age of seventeen. Soon thereafter, in the same year, I married my childhood sweetheart and we started our family. Becoming a nurse was even less likely now because I had the responsibility of caring for and raising three small children. My children were born close together. I got a job as a nurse's aide, but my dream was still intact.

Little did I know, Jesus Christ had a plan for my life also. Through a remarkable series of events, I began my journey toward my dream. I was the mother of three children with one more on the way when I started my college career. Situations that seem impossible to man are always possible with God. Man's impossibilities are God's opportunities!

My nursing profession is a gift to me from Jesus. I have always looked at it just like that. I ask myself these questions: how was I able to finance my schooling, how was I able to maintain an acceptable grade point average, how was I able to study, take care of a house, a husband, and four small children? It was nothing but a miracle! But, of course, Jesus is still in the miracle-working business. I give God all the honor and all the glory.

I graduated from Youngstown State University in 1973. What a joy! My dream had come true. The desire of my heart was now a reality. Jesus even blessed me to pass my state boards. Well, by now, I was ecstatic. I am still here at St. Elizabeth's because this is where Jesus wanted me. I have been here, come July, twenty-nine years. I have no desire to go elsewhere; I am content here. There have been many changes here, many ups and downs, but through it all, as the songwriter wrote, I have learned to trust in Jesus, I have learned to trust in God. Through it all, I learned to depend upon His Word. I learned that I can do all things through Christ who strengthens me. My attitude while I have been employed here, throughout the years, is that Jesus is my employer. Thinking that way makes me very careful about how I treat my patients and my coworkers, and about my day-to-day work ethics.

I pray that I have been pleasing and faithful to my Lord with the precious gift He has given me. Namely, to comfort those who are suffering, to wipe the tears of those who are weeping, to hold the hand of those who are fearful and trembling and, most of all, to lift high the name of Jesus, the Great Physician Himself! I truly enjoy my job here.

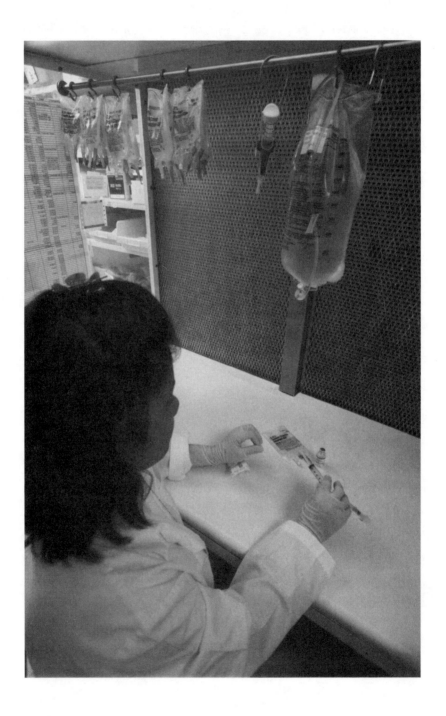

Thank
You Dad

by Patricia J. Feldhusem, RN—Rehab Unit
Marquette General Health Systems—Marquette, Michigan

"When I was growing up, I wanted to be a nurse because I wanted to help people. Today, I've been a nurse for thirty years and I smile when I recall the many times I've made my patients and their families feel better."

What is a hero? Someone who saves another… it could be a parent just doing what they do best: parenting. It could be a nurse, doing what they do best.

I think that all nurses have had cases that stand out in our minds for one reason or another. I know that one of the things that bothers EMTs is getting to the scene of an accident and finding a family member among the injured. For nurses and other health care providers, it is generally a lot easier to maintain your objectivity when your patient is someone you don't know. But when that patient is your dad…the whole spectrum changes.

It was difficult seeing him like that. My hero, my whole life. But he didn't want to go; he kept fighting. More than likely, he had some unfinished project tucked away somewhere that needed his attention. A cabinetmaker all his life, he was a contractor, and he also built houses, dug sewer lines, installed furnaces…he was a father, husband, township supervisor, lifelong Democrat and cemetery sexton.

The nurses were taking really good care of him and they were taking good care of me. While the patient is our primary concern, it often seems that the patient's family demands almost as much attention. Maybe demand is too harsh a word, but they need help too. They need help to deal with the situation. Who else can they talk to? Doctors can't be there twenty-four hours a day. . . nurses are. Some deal with it on their own terms…but they deal with it. And when they know you are one of them, maybe they step it up a little. Sitting back and watching the excellent care extended to my father made me realize just what an impact we do have on families. My dad was always proud that his two daughters were nurses and he let anyone and everyone know about it. That made me feel good, too, knowing how proud he was.

Thanks, Dad, for making me feel special.

Loyalty

by Nick Adams, Communications Writer
Wellmont Health System—Kingsport, Tennessee

"When I was growing up, I wanted to be a college graduate because, for me, that was a passport to a better life. Today, I am a dentist because I pursued my dream of being a better and more useful member of society."—Dr. Ed Hatcher

The influence of Dr. Ed Hatcher on the medical community of Northeast Tennessee is hard to quantify. A successful dentist for more than thirty years in Bristol, Tennessee, Dr. Hatcher was also instrumental in the creation of the area's only medical school and the region's first comprehensive health planning agency.

Dr. Hatcher would qualify as an everyday hero if he had done nothing after his retirement, but the results of his past labor continue to return dividends. He has been anything but idle, serving on the Wellmont Health System Board of Directors, the Wellmont Bristol Regional Medical Center Board of Directors, the Personnel Committee of the Wellmont Board and the Wellmont Quality Integration Committee.

Dr. Hatcher's influence isn't just limited to the Tri-Cities region—or the United States for that matter.

The small Asian country of Bangladesh is one of the world's poorest nations, a fact that came to Dr. Hatcher's attention near the time that Bristol Memorial Hospital was making way for Bristol Regional Medical Center.

"The people of that country need help—anything you can do for them," Dr. Hatcher said. "I knew there was going to be some outdated or unused medical equipment. That made me realize I could get involved and build something substantial."

Dr. Hatcher petitioned the members of what would become the Wellmont Bristol Regional Board of Directors and was given enough equipment and supplies to start a seventy-five bed hospital in Jessore, Bangladesh, a city he has now visited several times.

The experience led Dr. Hatcher to continue his overseas work and also helped found a medical clinic and dental clinic in Quezon City in the Philippines.

But some of the most important work done by Dr. Hatcher was one of the most beneficial to the medical community of the Tri-Cities.

After realizing that many students from northeast Tennessee and southwest Virginia were forced to travel hundreds of miles to attend medical school, Dr. Hatcher and several other volunteers formed the Appalachian Center for the Healing Arts, which became the body responsible for issuing certificates of need in Tennessee before the establishment of the Health Facilities Commission.

Demographics collected by ARCHA showed that there was good reason to pursue the idea of developing a medical school in Johnson City, and Dr. Hatcher was active in the early efforts to organize the James H. Quillen College of Medicine at East Tennessee State University.

Though Dr. Hatcher's career has actually had global influence, he says he is proudest of the fact that the majority of his dental patients moved their business to his daughter's practice after his retirement.

"The patients appreciated the care I gave them," Dr. Hatcher said. "They wouldn't have stayed loyal if I hadn't done my job right."

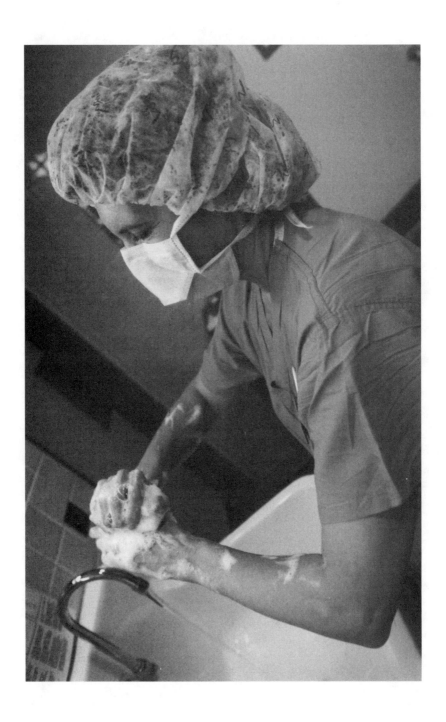

11 a.m.

by Andrea Posey, RN, MSN, Academic Coordinator
University of Alaska School of Nursing—Anchorage, Alaska

"When I was growing up, I wanted to be a veterinarian because I wanted to help God's smallest creatures. Today, I am a nurse and I help God's greatest creatures… people."

Mr. O was not a very nice person. In fact, he had been in trouble with the police on many occasions. Finally, his lifestyle caught up with him and he was critically injured by a rusty knife. Now he lay restrained in a bed on my critical care unit. Nobody really wanted to care for Mr. O because of the horrible things he had done. Most felt he deserved his fate. For some reason, I didn't mind caring for him and I requested him for a patient almost every shift I worked.

Mr. O was one of those intensive care unit patients who was always having an emergency… a bleeder would just spring up, arrhythmias would suddenly occur, or he would lapse back into sepsis. Still, he hung on day after day. And I cared for him, day after day. I looked into his green eyes and saw him for the person he was, aside from what he had done. I could see sadness, pain and fear. Wanting to help him come to terms with his predicament, I was able to find a priest to spend time with him. Mr. O wrote the priest a note and said he knew God had forgiven him and he was ready to die.

A week later, I was working a double shift, from evening to night and, as usual, I had Mr. O for my patient. Not far into the evening, he sprung a massive GI bleed. For hours I stood at his bedside lavaging his NG tube with iced water and Maalox. Still, bright red blood continued to spew from his tube. The interns and residents were called and gathered around deciding what to do.

"Let's take him to surgery and explore to find the cause of this bleed," one said.

"I know an experimental therapy that might work," said another. On and on they discussed. On and on Mr. O bled until finally he was in hypovolemic shock. I was exhausted and my nerves were ragged.

"He is ready to die," I told the interns. "He has made his peace. Let him go."

But that was not an option. Death would mean they had failed.

Finally, I began yelling at them. "You can't treat him like a guinea pig! He is a person who is suffering! Just make him comfortable and let him go!"

But again, that was not an option. Finally, the hellish shift ended and I went home. Mr. O was still alive and still bleeding.

That morning, something woke me from my fitful slumber. There at the end of my bed stood Mr. O, pale and transparent. I could see his lips forming the words "Thank you." I jumped up and really woke up now. Realizing it was just a dream, I rolled over to go back to sleep. I looked at the clock: it read 11a.m.

That afternoon, as I started my evening shift, I noticed Mr. O's bed was empty.

"When did he die?" I asked.

"At exactly 11 a.m.," replied my coworker.

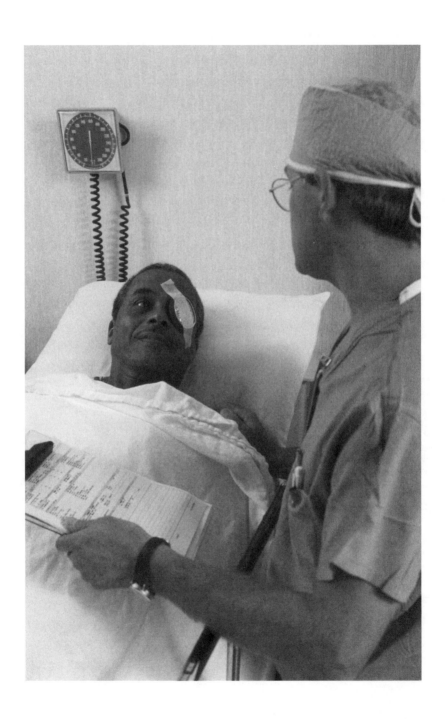

Empire State
Building

by Toni L. Woods, Hospitality Manager
Lenox Hill Hospital—New York, New York

"When I was growing up, I wanted to be a doctor because I wanted to help heal people and to make them feel better. Today, I am like a doctor because I am able to spend quality time with patients when they are at their most vulnerable and that in itself can help them heal or just make them feel better."

As a hospitality manager, I've encountered many situations where I've humbly become the eyes, ears, nose, mouth, or arms and legs of my patients. These occasions have ranged from looking for a misplaced pair of glasses to listening to concerned family members and relaying their messages to my patients, to reading the details of the hospice where someone has chosen to spend their final hours. When I received a phone call from my nurse manager with a most unusual request, the first thing that came to mind was my three-year-old daughter and the immeasurable love I feel for her.

The message began with the diagnosis, prognosis and age of the patient. With this information I knew there was no time to spare. Chemotherapy treatment was needed as soon as possible, but over this lay the cloud of possible sterility. The ray of hope presented by my nurse lay in the possibility of harvesting some of our patient's reproductive cells so that the patient could focus all of his energy on beating the odds. I jumped on the worldwide web, knowing that this would be my quickest source of information. In seconds, there were lists of clinics that could preserve the cells until such a time as my patient might decide to begin that chapter of his life.

Together with my nurse manager, we began a series of phone calls collecting information and details of the procedure that would be necessary to collect the sample so it would be viable and storable. We were on a mission; not an ordinary mission, but a mission of love and hope for the future and for future generations. We enlisted the help of a second nurse manager, who provided a location that was both private and sterile where the harvesting could occur. She also extended herself enough to go to the corner bookstore to purchase materials that would be conducive to the harvest.

We led my patient to the room, and with nervous apprehension, he thanked us for all that we had done. It seemed small in comparison with all that he had faced in the previous forty-eight hours and the road that lay ahead.

A final phone call was made to the storage center to get the instructions and directions, and to my surprise, "350 Fifth Avenue" turned out to be the Empire State Building. My heart sank. Less than a week before, I tearfully watched my innocence destroyed with the leveling of the Twin Towers. There was no way to know if there would be another terrorist attack, but everyone speculated that the Empire State Building would be a target for its staunch representation of New York. I then made two additional phone calls, one to the daycare center where my daughter spends her days, and another to my boyfriend, and the last leg of the journey was to begin.

The specimen had to be maintained at body temperature and the delivery must be made in less than one hour after the harvest. Quickly, we wrapped the sterile container in a towel and blanket and off I went. The line to enter the Empire State Building ran down Fifth Avenue and down 34th Street. Anxiously, I made my way to the security desk staring at my watch the entire way, watching the minutes quickly run down, and with them the hope of getting to the center in time to preserve the sample. The chemotherapy treatments had begun so this had to be a successful trip. With ten minutes remaining, I made it to the security desk where there was a minor roadblock of how the package would be inspected. I insisted that it should not go through the X-ray machine for fear that this might damage the specimen. Finally, another inspector agreed to inspect it manually and I arrived at the bank with just five minutes to spare. The paperwork was processed and the trip was a success.

I hope that one day my patient will know the joys of extending unconditional love in such a special way. I hope he will find himself holding a child, something so small that will forever change his life and infuse it with the unexplainable sensations only felt when holding new life in your hands; a life that you have helped to be.

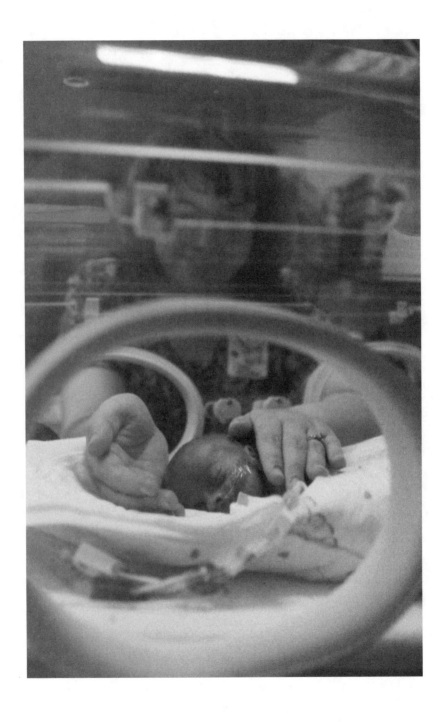

A Nurse's Story

by Teresa R. Renninger, RN, BSN, TCCN—SICU
St. Elizabeth Health Center—Youngstown, Ohio

"When I was growing up, I wanted to be a caregiver, nurse, or teacher because I felt this was where the greatest need existed. There just could not be any more rewarding place to be than in helping others get well, recover and go on with their lives. Today I am a nurse and teacher because I am always challenged with new ideas and ways to help others feel complete. I feel very blessed with many talents that have come out in times of need to help people and their families in whatever way it takes to extend the feeling of love, care and blessings to each of them."

Once there was a little girl who began her life feeling everything around her was pretty special. The feeling inside her was that God must have sent her to earth for some very special reason. The life around her was special. Life itself was precious. Every minute of every day was exciting because there was so much to learn about and experience in the world that surrounded her. The smells of the changing seasons were special, the wind or breeze blowing through her hair, the soft touch of rose petals, the beautiful colors of the different flowers, the fact that she could speak two languages and understand two or three others, were all so special. It was a wonderful feeling to be of Spanish heritage and be able to communicate with people of various cultures. It was truly a learning experience, something she was very proud of having the ability to do.

Life was beautiful no matter how mean some people could be to one another. From a very young age, this little girl prayed every day that things would change and people would think better of themselves as well as others. There had to be something she could do to make things better. There just had to be a way. She made up her mind to learn as much as possible and to use herself as a good example; hopefully the rest would follow. She kept her mouth shut and ears open to absorb as much as possible from everything around her wherever she went.

Things were not always good at home. Her mother was a mean and abusive person who frightened her very much. However, she kept praying to God for a better place to live with a better way of life someday. She took the abuse and only returned love. God was her strength and prayers her fuel. With the lack of maternal love from her mother and being raised by her grandmother, she soon learned to feel love for anyone who was different, rejected, unfortunate, maimed, handicapped, or treated cruelly. She always had love, kindness, concern and understanding for others. It was fascinating to see just how people managed to get through each day with their afflictions. Living in Brooklyn, New York, and walking those streets, riding the trains or buses, you saw an awful lot right in front of you without having to seek it out. Some things were frightening, some pitiful, others sad, yet others ugly or mean. There were many maltreated, homeless, impaired or disabled people in the world.

In play, she pretended to be caring for these people, using her dolls, stuffed animals, and teddy bears. She would cook for them, wash their clothes, give them first aid, keep them warm, read stories to them, sing to them and rock them to sleep. She was always giving plenty of kindness, tenderness and love. Her grandmother even played at times as one of the caregivers who made doll clothes and bandages, crocheted blankets, and provided Jell-O, cookies, juice, and tiny sandwiches for the children in the orphanage or hospital. At times, Grandma would sing in Spanish to the children. This was the beginning of a lifetime of caring for others for this child.

At age eight, the little girl was hospitalized for appendicitis, and her appendix burst while being removed. She was in the hospital for quite awhile and made friends with several nurses. One day she told one nurse of her dream to become a nurse when she grew up. The nurse began taking her on rounds once the girl was able to be up in a wheelchair and even showed her the medicine room where the drugs were dispensed in cups. By the end of her stay in the hospital, this little girl knew her dream of becoming a nurse just had to become a reality. How proud she was of those nurses.

In the meantime, Grandma began to run her home as a foster home for older adults who needed someplace to stay, but were not ready to be placed in a nursing home or hospital. They needed to be watched and could no longer live alone. Some did not want to live alone and wanted companionship. What a wonderful thing Grandma was doing. Her uncle lived at home and helped also.

The little girl soon began helping as part of her chores. Duties consisted of folding clothes, helping to clean up the rooms, changing linens, getting meal trays ready, and carrying trays up to the people who could not come down for meals. She also assisted those who could come down. After supper and homework, they played cards, checkers and other games. It was a great experience and a wonderful opportunity for learning more about people. Grandma loved them all and cried whenever we lost one. She had such love for people and everyone loved her.

The child in this story grew up to become a nurse. That nurse is me. My grandmother wanted me to be a schoolteacher, but I wanted to be a nurse. So one day we compromised when I told her that someday I would be a teacher of nursing. Her eyes welled up with tears and she beamed with pride.

I have been a nurse for twenty-seven years. Starting out as a nurse's aide for three years, I went on to become an LPN for ten years. I then pursued my RN and now I have completed my BSN. Nurses come from all walks of life and all have their own reasons for entering nursing. As for myself, I feel I was born to become a nurse. I could never see myself as anything else. Nothing could ever be as rewarding or satisfying as helping someone in need. It provides personal fulfillment and the rewards are many.

Nursing is something very special and not everyone can do it. It requires a lot of personal sacrificing of time, energy, and sleep. The demands are often highly stressful. Nurses are at the bedside around the clock, sometimes continuously, depending on how critical a patient is; yet the importance of our hard work is not appreciated. This is why I would like to be a part of helping nurses be seen for what they really are and their true worth. We are constantly making critical decisions in critical situations and we should be acknowledged for our expertise and respected for our knowledge. We should always want to be better than we are and not settle for anything less.

Professionalism takes hard work and it is an ongoing process. More nurses need to realize this and band together with those of us who do because this is the only way we will be seen, heard and recognized as the special group of professionals we are.

Nursing is a commitment. We need to respect ourselves and what we represent before we can expect others to respect us. Respect is earned. There are many challenges ahead of us in nursing with all the changes coming about in the world of health care. I hope I can be a part of them in one way or another. I hope I can continue to help make a difference.

Eventually, I hope to go on for my masters and teach nursing. This continues to be my dream. After all, I have a promise to fulfill. Lord willing, it will happen.

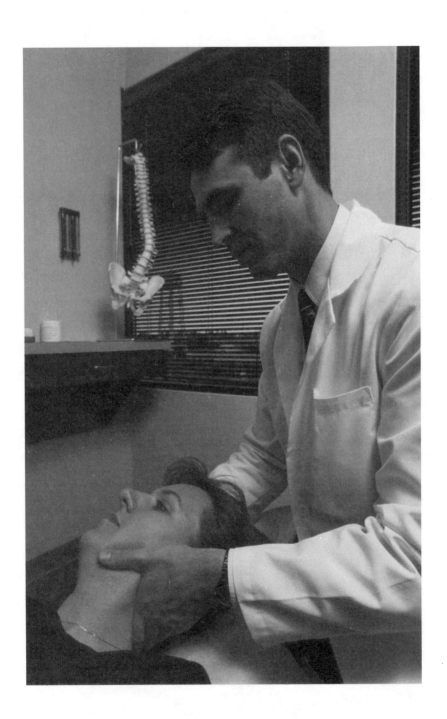

In Your Blood

by Chris Martini, RN—Heart and Vascular Services
St. Elizabeth Health Center—Youngstown, Ohio

"I don't believe a person chooses nursing as a career. I believe it chooses you. Nursing is something that is in your blood. It is a desire to wake up each day knowing what you do matters—a chance to make a difference in someone's life. It is not a job you can perfect, but a continual learning process. Each day you can learn something to improve your skills as a nurse or your compassion as a person."

Nursing is the privilege of holding a person's hand as they take their final breath and of handing a new mother her baby for the first time. It is the fulfillment you feel when you struggle to keep a patient alive for twelve hours and then know they've improved when you leave at the end of your shift. It is the joy you feel when those patients *walk* back into your unit months later and say, "thank you," and the tears you shed with countless families over the patients you lose.

Nursing is tired feet and aching backs. It is countless times you have "tucked in" your children over the phone because you're working overtime. It is the ability to convince yourself a bag of pretzels and a Diet Coke outside your patient's room is a healthy meal. Nursing is spending numerous holidays and weekends at work instead of with your family. It is the frustration of working short-staffed and the pride you feel when you make it through the shift.

It is knowing, through the good and bad, that there is nothing you'd rather do than be a NURSE!

I am a Nurse

by Mary Ann Minick, RN—Perinatal Education
St. Joseph Health Center—Warren, Ohio

"Why did I become a nurse? I feel I was born a nurse. Nursing is not a job; it's a way of life. It defines who I am. It's my philosophy of life. Nursing is caring, sharing, giving and loving mankind. It's touching people soul to soul. It's seeing the reflection of Christ in others."

Nursing isn't an eight-hour shift, it's 24/7. Nursing encompasses my whole life. I nurse my family, my friends, my patients, and all my acquaintances.

Nursing may not be the most prestigious or highest-paying position in life, but it is without a doubt the most rewarding. The reward is in the hearts of those I've touched by being who *I am, a nurse*.

# of a Hero
Definition

by Kelley MacDonald, Central Billing Office
Marquette General Health System—Marquette, Michigan

The hero in this story would never call herself a hero, only someone who did what she knew how to do when another was in need. I think that is a pretty good definition of a hero.

A small boy about four years old was out sledding with his family when a parent's worst nightmare happened. The boy collided head first with another sledder. It was more than a thirty-minute drive to the nearest hospital, but the child was conscious so his parents decided to drive him to the hospital. At some point during the ride, the boy lost consciousness. His parents decided they could not get him to the hospital fast enough and decided to stop and call an ambulance at this point. They were on an area of M-553 that has many homes.

I believe that angels were watching that little one because the home where his parents chose to stop for help contained a hero. The woman living in that home had twenty years of medical experience, first as an EMT, and later as an X-ray tech at Marquette General Hospital. Plus the nerves of steel needed to think in a very bad situation. As her husband and the boy's father called an ambulance, the woman went to the truck to see if she could help.

What she saw in the truck was a boy not only unconscious, but not breathing. I don't know for sure why the child stopped breathing, but I know that it would have taken about ten minutes for the nearest ambulance to get to him. Because of the skills of the woman in that home, a little boy's life was saved. She knew CPR and all the other skills necessary to get that boy breathing again.

At work the next day, the woman went to see that boy in the intensive care unit. He was bouncing on his bed like nothing ever happened. In a terrible moment, that family met one of God's angels on earth. I know that the family of that boy would call her a hero. I always knew she was because she is mine too (well, most days)…she is my mother, Shevawn MacDonald.

'Til the End

by Terri E. May, Long-Term Care
Seneca Health District—Chester, California

"**I** never get tired of the warm feeling I get when I see the smile of recognition from the cloudy eyes of the lost. They do come back every now and then. They love to see people they remember. They pat your hand and nod. The twisted old fingers cling tightly, begging for just a minute longer. They nod as we rush away down the hall for a sweater and a book. They know we'll be back. We won't forget them. They know that we'll be there until the end."

Wiping another tear from my cheek, nodding, a smile here, a wave there. I look around the funeral chapel. I see two of my co-workers making their way through the crowd. Another service

121

for one of the "forgotten." Forgotten it seems, until the funeral; then they will remember. It's a way of life in our world. We take care of them until they are called home. Then we say our public goodbyes. Sometimes we get a special hug because some of the family knew we were there, loving and caring to the very end: we, the people of long-term care. We are the unseen, unsung heroes, forever working behind the scenes to make sure that Nanna looks her best for Aunt Millie when she shows up clucking, "It's a shame you had to put her here, tsk, tsk, what a shame."

We are the women and men the aged and dying see every day. We bathe them and comb their hair. We dress them and feed them. We potty and wipe, we clean their eyes and wipe their noses. We shave them and brush their teeth. We do for them what they can no longer do for themselves. We do for them what families can no longer do at home. We take them in and slowly, but surely, fall in love. We love them and we love our jobs. We must, or we couldn't keep coming back. It is grueling work, hard and unforgiving, often unnoticed and even more often, looked down upon by the rest of the medical community. We don't have the glory of the ER or the drama of surgery. We don't even have the anticipation of OB. We just are. We rush the oxygen concentrators behind the wheelchairs while carrying the walker after we finish shower number two. We plot shower number three while we potty 14A after walking 9B, knowing all the time that 5B will be ringing again for no apparent reason. Day after day, we race along, taking care of our people, loving our jobs and doing that something extra because nobody else will. We are our patients' lives. A lot of the time we are all they have left. Family is too far away, friends long since gone.

When one of our ladies was too sick to go out and get her hair done, we brought the salon to her. We washed her hair with a shampoo cap, then dried it, set it, curled it, ratted it and combed it. We did her makeup and we watched her glow. That simple act of kindness meant the world to that woman. We gave of ourselves because we could. That's what heroes do. They give of themselves simply because they can. Lord knows we don't do what we do every shift to be noticed. Who would ever know or care, for that matter? We get very little recognition from our patients' families or friends. Very few even make their way in anymore. The rest of our nursing counterparts would rather die than spend a shift in *long term.* "What a loss," I say. What a loss, they will never get to know these wonderful old people. People who still have a story to tell. What a shame that they never get to stop and hold the hand of a lonely soul. What a loss to miss out on the last day of someone's life. What a shame to let it all pass by.

I never get tired of the warm feeling I get when I see a smile of recognition from the cloudy eyes of the lost. They do come back every now and then. They love to see people they remember. They pat your hand and nod. The twisted old fingers cling tightly, begging for just a minute longer. They nod as we rush away down the hall for a sweater and a book. They know we'll be back. We won't forget them. They know that we'll be there until the end.

The pastor was finishing, "If anyone has a special memory or a story, please stand and share it with us now." We looked at each other through tear-filled eyes, sitting there in that small funeral chapel. We have enough memories and stories to fill a million books. If only one page for each we've lost. Knowing and caring 'til the end, we are the heroes of long-term care.

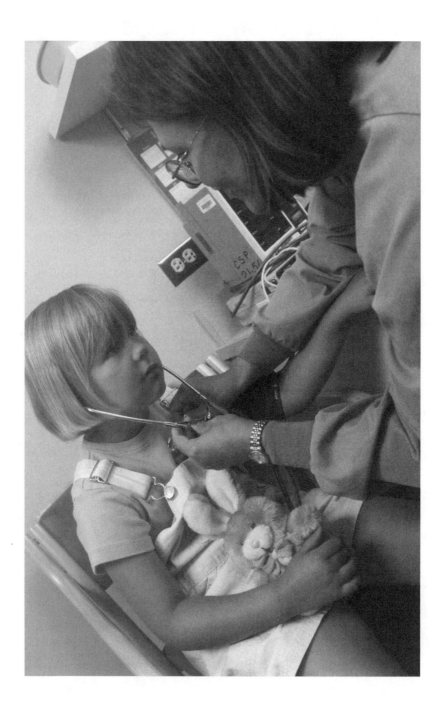

Hey Nurse, That Is a Pink Pig on Your Head?

by Pam Adams, RN
Valley View Medical Center—Paragonah, Utah

John, a nurse at our hospital, has a mother who makes animal print head covers for his baseball cap—some of these have a Dalmatian print with ears that hang down, some are jungle animals, etc. John's mother also made him some headbands (the plastic kind) with three-dimensional animals on them to wear to work to entertain sick kids. But I think he felt a little funny wearing a plastic headband. So one night on the graveyard shift, his wife, a respiratory therapist, brought the headbands for us girls to use. One of the headbands (my favorite) had a pink pig and the other had Tigger from *Winnie the Pooh*. Well, naturally, we put them on right away; I mean, after all, we are the night shift!

Things were going right along in the ICU until a nurse named Rick on the med/surg floor started yelling down the hall into the ICU for me to come quick to room 10. I picked up the IV pole and ran to room 10 where the patient, an eighty-year-old woman, had pulled out her IV, then picked up the IV pole and sent it sailing through the plate glass window. After this, she got naked, and pulled out her Foley catheter and tied it around her waist. She now was standing by the bed, all eighty pounds of naked glory, with two glass shards, one in each hand, and the Foley tied around her waist.

The security guy arrived at the same time I did, and she yelled at him, "Get out of here!" He slammed the door to room 10 and cowered by it. My concern was that she would try to crawl out the shattered window, dragging the Foley collection bag with her. She wasn't going to reason with any of us.

So I called the boys in blue, the city police. Four of them came storming in, stretching their gloves on as they ran down the hall. They paused and looked at me quite curiously before opening the door to room 10.

The patient was relieved to see the police there to take care of her. After all, we were the obvious bad guys. They distracted her by pretending to make a phone call and then got her into a patient gown and settled into a new room. By then she was reoriented and knew what had happened. But neither she nor we knew why she had become so confused and agitated.

The blood on and around her fortunately was solely from the IV that she pulled out. Miraculously, she received no cuts from the shattered glass.

The police gave me another very curious look and then left. It was shortly after that when I realized I had a pink pig on top of my head.

Team
Makes
Gift of
Life Possible

by Bob Stronach, Public Relations Director
St. Elizabeth Medical Center—Utica, New York

"Phenomenal support" in a difficult situation was the way the Center for Donation & Transplant described the medical staff at St. Elizabeth Medical Center Utica, New York.

"They were so professional and, most importantly, so compassionate to the (organ donor) family and to the hospital staff," said Joey Nuqui, Organ Procurement Coordinator for the Albany, New York, transplant center. "They were instrumental in making something good come out of a tragic event—saving the lives of transplant recipients."

It began with neurosurgeon W.G. Rusyniak, MD, on call for his partners on the evening of July 24, 2002, who went out of his way to come into the medical center to talk to the family about the patient's status.

"He was very supportive of the entire process and told us to call him anytime if we needed him," noted Nuqui.

Next, neurologist A. Shatla, MD, came into the intensive care unit to do the clinical evaluation of brain death and to read the EEG.

"He was kind enough to accommodate us as quickly as possible because we were on time constraint with the status of the organs," Nuqui said.

Then anesthesiologist S. Motta, MD, placed the arterial line and CVP line to facilitate monitoring and access. But midnight was approaching and, in order to place the heart for transplant, an echocardiogram was needed. A call went out to cardiologist P. Varma, MD, who showed up in less than half an hour.

"His cheerfulness despite the time of night boosted the morale of the staff," noted Nuqui.

Emergency physician John Rubin, DO, took the time to read some X-rays despite a hectic night in the emergency department. Finally, anesthesiologists A. Reddy, MD, and C. Cozza, MD, provided anesthesia during the process.

"These doctors show their humanity by being there when needed," Nuqui said in a letter to St. Elizabeth medical director, Albert D'Accurzio, MD. "They gave excellent health care and did it with compassion and respect for the dignity of all, which is your hospital's mission statement. Your community is blessed with such physicians. They were part of a wonderful team that made the gift of life possible."

The Last
Flight

by Pam Adams, RN
Valley View Medical Center—Paragonah, Utah

A couple of years ago, I came into work on graveyard shift in the intensive care unit. My patient that night, and for the next several nights, was a sixty-two-year-old woman, Mrs. R. She had been admitted with congestive heart failure. We would find out over the next few days that she in fact had metastatic cancer that had progressed to her lungs and was thus the reason for the congestive heart failure.

Amazingly enough, Mrs. R. had a strong, quiet resolve about her diagnosis and poor prognosis. However, her family, particularly the children and her physician did not share her sentiment.

In the several days that followed, both the physician and her children were angry and sometimes quite pushy about insisting that Mrs. R. was only sixty-two, she had several small grandchildren and her youngest daughter was in her ninth month of pregnancy.

The next time I came to work, Mrs. R. was much more debilitated physically. Her respirations were rapid and shallow. Her face was gray. The oxygen saturation was steadily trending down. Her family was at her side, holding her hand, watching her with hope and fear; hope that somehow she could stay just a little longer, maybe just until the new grandbaby was born, and fear that she could not.

It was now three o'clock. I was in the ICU, and Vivian observed the scene for a few minutes, and then she said, "You know, she's bought the ticket."

I said, "What ticket?"

Viv said, "She's bought the plane ticket, and even though the airport is fogged in, the airplane is still going to take off." Shortly after our conversation, Mrs. R. expired.

In this life, whether we are doctors, nurses or family members, we need to hold our patient's hand while they walk down the gate, board the plane and take the "last flight."

Customer
Service
Shines
at Unity Health

by Elisa Loomis, Human Resources Coordinator
and Terry Seiler, Public Relations Assistant
Unity Health—Rochester, New York

Since the human resources department at Unity Health is so focused on customer service, we thought you would be interested in learning that they really do practice what they preach.

This is a great team of people I work with in human resources. I seriously injured my knee awhile back, so I was unable to walk. However, I returned to Unity Health using a combination of wheelchair and walker.

During this time, coworkers sent cards, gifts, and home-cooked meals; did chores such as housekeeping, laundry and cooking for me; ran to the grocery, banking and post office errands; and chauffeured me to and from work, doctor's and physical therapy appointments, and anywhere else I needed to go.

They offered this kindness in spite of their long work hours, commitments to their children's activities or to elderly parents, and all of the other juggling of their own hectic lives. I have never worked with such thoughtful, supportive and compassionate people. After giving of themselves all day to our many employees and managers, they went the extra mile to take care of one of their own. I am privileged to work beside them and I wanted you to know how they truly epitomize service to the customer!

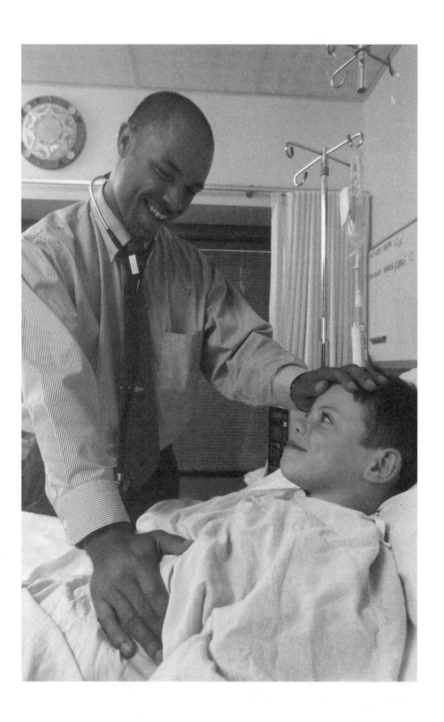

Plain Jane

by Eileen R. Meehan, Patient Relations Representative
The Hospital of Saint Raphael—New Haven, Connecticut

"Maybe the cruel disease of Alzheimer's has a hidden gift that no one knows about. Maybe these patients learn the secret of life or meet a spiritual being, or maybe they are God's angels on earth. I guess we will never know."

He sat still and silent, but he had a swashbuckling grin on his face. He was at one time a very good-looking man, but now he was reduced to being tethered to a chair, wearing only a jonnie-coat and an adult-size diaper. He had the most beautiful skin I had ever seen. His cheeks were brushed with roses and his eyes…his eyes were deep, lost, and yet very kind. This man that I will call Ben was in the advanced stages of early-onset Alzheimer's and his condition was indeed terminal.

As a patient representative, I visit many patients in any given day, and on this day, I had the unforgettable experience of meeting Ben.

At first I didn't even notice him. I was walking by him on my way to meet with another patient when his restrained hand reached out for my arm. I stopped and he said, "Plain Jane." My first thought was, "Wow, this really is a bad hair day," and my second thought was: "How funny are you?" "Okay," I said, "Now that you have my attention, what can I do for you, good-looking?" He just looked at me, not staring, just gazing; gazing at what felt like my soul. I was not even a little offended because he wasn't looking for beauty or my dress size; he was just looking. (Let's not forget, we already established that I'm "Plain Jane.")

One of the nurses approached me and said: "Hey, Ei (short for Eileen), you probably won't get much feedback from Ben because he's at the end of a short fight with Alzheimer's." I asked if I could sit with him for a minute since I didn't know if he was prone to agitation or not, and she said, "Go ahead, he won't remember you ten minutes from now anyway."

I sat with Ben for over an hour. I couldn't possibly tell you what we talked about because he was really confused. I do know that, to this day, no one has ever looked at me with the same kind of peace in their eyes that he had. Maybe the cruel disease of Alzheimer's has a hidden gift that no one knows about. Maybe these patients learn the secret of life or meet a spiritual being, or maybe they are God's angels on earth. I guess we will never know.

A month went by and Ben was still hanging on. I hadn't seen him since our first meeting. One of the nurses told me the end was very near. Knowing that he was going to die very soon, I decided to say goodbye. I knew he would not remember me, but I still felt the need to see him one last time. I walked into his room where his family sat at his bedside. There he lay, still and silent, with that swashbuckling grin on his face, and with those peaceful eyes, his quivering voice said, "Hi, Plain Jane."

Those three words bring me sanity on a bad day, and make me laugh on a sad day. I will always be thankful to Ben. I will never forget him as he did not forget me.

Chris Thrash, author of *Everyday Heroes*, is a health care consultant and motivational speaker for hospitals. His tremendous expertise in patient and employee satisfaction turnaround has assisted hospitals across the nation in developing successful service cultures. Chris is also a dynamic keynote speaker for conferences and meetings. If you would like information about possibly bringing Chris to your organization, please contact:

Harvington Media, Inc.
4500 West Illinois Avenue, Suite 116
Midland, Texas 79703
Phone: (800) 733-7008
E-mail: chris@harvingtonmedia.com
Website: www.christhrash.com

To order additional copies of this book, *Everyday Heroes*, contact Harvington Media at the address and/or phone number listed above.

Looking *for* Great Training Videos *to Motivate and Inspire the* Heroes at Your Hospital?

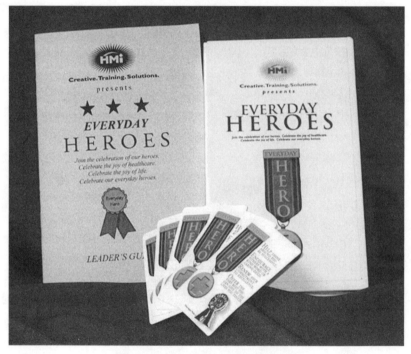

EVERYDAY HEROES

This best-selling video inspires hospital staff members to look at what they do with a whole new perspective. Health care workers are special people who give of themselves to make a difference, a real difference in the lives of others every day. You might call them "Everyday Heroes." *Running time: 15 minutes.*

Available for purchase or rental. To order a free 14-day preview, call 1-800-733-7008.

SMILE: You're on Customer Camera

(featuring Chris Thrash as the narrator)

(Healthcare Version) This dynamic video program introduces key concepts of customer service that will re-energize staff members as they are taken on a humorous tour of the hospital seen through the patient's eyes. The creator of this exciting training program actually took a hospital that was struggling with patient satisfaction and moved that organization into one of the top 75 hospitals in the nation. *Running time: 10 minutes.*

Available for purchase or rental. To order a free 14-day preview, call 1-800-733-7008.

PRIDE: What Does Exceptional Service Look and Sound Like?

(featuring Chris Thrash as the narrator)

What does excellent service look and sound like? This film is based on the PRIDE Initiative from Lehigh Valley Health Network in eastern Pennsylvania known nationally for clinical innovation and service excellence. Lehigh Valley's PRIDE Initiative is featured in Disney's new book, *Be Our Guest*, as a best practice in how to define and describe what exceptional service looks and sounds like in a health care setting.

Available for purchase or rental. To order a
free 14-day preview, call 1-800-733-7008.